Live

as Jesus Lived

BOOK 2 EXPERIENCE THE LIFE

Live
as Jesus Lived

Transformed Character

BILL HULL & PAUL MASCARELLA

NAVPRESS

Discipleship Inside Out™

Discipleship Inside Out™

NavPress is the publishing ministry of The Navigators, an international Christian organization and leader in personal spiritual development. NavPress is committed to helping people grow spiritually and enjoy lives of meaning and hope through personal and group resources that are biblically rooted, culturally relevant, and highly practical.

**For a free catalog go to www.NavPress.com
or call 1.800.366.7788 in the United States or 1.800.839.4769 in Canada.**

ISBN-13: 978-1-61521-541-6

Cover design by Arvid Wallen
Cover image by Shutterstock

Unless otherwise identified, all Scripture quotations in this publication are taken from the *Holy Bible, New International Version®* (NIV®). Copyright © 1973, 1978, 1984 by International Bible Society. Used by permission of Zondervan. All rights reserved. Other versions used include: *The Living Bible* (TLB), copyright © 1971, used by permission of Tyndale House Publishers, Inc., Wheaton, IL 60189, all rights reserved; the *Holy Bible*, New Living Translation (NLT), copyright © 1996, 2004. Used by permission of Tyndale House Publishers, Inc., Wheaton, Illinois 60189. All rights reserved; the New American Standard Bible® (NASB), copyright © 1960, 1962, 1963, 1968, 1971, 1972, 1973, 1975, 1977, 1995 by The Lockman Foundation. Used by permission; and the King James Version (KJV).

Printed in the United States of America

1 2 3 4 5 6 7 8 / 14 13 12 11 10

CONTENTS

INTRODUCTION

To *experience the life* is to commit to a way or pattern of life. Its basis is humility and it is a life of self-denial and submission to others. The life that Jesus lived and prescribed for us is different from the one being offered by many churches. His servant leadership was radically distinct from what is extolled by secular society and even too bold for what is modeled in the Christian community. This life is essentially the *faith of following*, of taking up one's cross daily and following Him. It is fundamentally about giving up the right to run your own life. It is living the life that Jesus lived, the life to which He has called every disciple.

To put it another way, we can only experience the life Jesus has called us to by committing to training that will enable us to believe as Jesus believed, live as Jesus lived, love as Jesus loved, minister as Jesus ministered, and lead as Jesus led.

It is only by taking Jesus' discipling yoke upon ourselves that we can experience the life that Jesus lived. Only then will we discover its light burden and enjoy His promised "rest for our souls" (Matthew 11:29-30).

ABOUT THIS BOOK

This book is the second in the five-book EXPERIENCE THE LIFE series. It continues the thirty-week course, built upon the ideas introduced and developed in Bill Hull's book *Choose the Life,* which begins with the series' first book, *Believe as Jesus Believed.*

Its Purpose

EXPERIENCE THE LIFE exists to assist the motivated disciple in entering into a more profound way of thinking and living. That way is the pattern of life Jesus modeled and then called every interested person to follow. Simply put, it is the living out of Jesus' life by: believing as Jesus believed, living as Jesus lived, loving as Jesus loved, ministering as Jesus ministered, and leading as Jesus led. This *Life* is a life grounded in humility—characterized by submission, obedience, suffering, and the joys of exaltation. It is the life that transforms its adherents and penetrates the strongest resistance. It then calls upon each person to rethink what it means to be a follower of Jesus.

This book is the second in the five-book EXPERIENCE THE LIFE series. It is designed to lead disciples in a thirty-week course, built upon the ideas introduced and developed in Bill Hull's book *Choose the Life.* It provides a daily format that directs a disciple's thinking toward the application of these truths, thereby producing in him a faith hospitable to healthy spiritual transformation—*a faith that embraces discipleship.*

Its Participants

Virtually all significant change can, should be, and eventually is tested in relationship to others. To say that one is more loving without it being verified in relation to others is hollow. Not only do others need to be involved to test one's progress, they are needed to encourage and help someone else in the journey of transformation. Therefore, going on the journey with others is absolutely necessary.

The five books are designed to lead each disciple in a personal journey of spiritual formation by participation within a community of disciples, who have likewise decided to *experience the life.*

The community is composed of (optimally) from two to eight disciples being led in this thirty-week course to *experience the life.*

Participants in the community agree to make time and perform the daily assignments as directed in each book. They have agreed to pray daily for the other members of their community and to keep whatever is shared at their community meeting in confidence. They will attend and fully participate in each weekly community meeting.

Its Process

We recognize that all change, all spiritual transformation, is the result of a process. Events may instigate change in people; they may provide the motive, the occasion, and the venue for change to begin, but the changes that result in healthy spiritual transformation are the product of a process.

We can glean a description of the transformational process from the apostle Paul's command in Romans 12:2:

> Do not conform any longer to the pattern of this world, but be transformed by the renewing of your mind. Then you will be able to test and approve what God's will is—his good, pleasing and perfect will.

This process of transformation asserts that the believer must no longer conform to what is false, the "pattern of this world" (its ideas and values, and the behaviors which express them). Also, he must be transformed, which means his pattern must be changed, conformed to another pattern (the truth), which is not "of this world." This is done by the process of "the renewing of your mind." What does it mean to renew something? To what is Paul referring when he says that the mind must undergo this renewal?

To renew something means to act upon something in ways that will cause it to be as it was when it was new. The principle idea is one of restoring something that is currently malfunctioning and breaking down to its fully functioning state, its original pristine state, the state it was in prior to it sustaining any damage. We must avoid the modern notion that renewing something means simply replacing the old thing with an entirely new thing. Paul, and the people to whom he wrote these words, would simply not understand *renew* to mean anything like what we moderns mean when we use the word *replace*. They would understand that renewing the wheels on one's cart meant repairing them to their fully functioning state. And so, what Paul means by "being transformed by the *renewing* of your mind" (emphasis ours) is that the mind must undergo changes, repairs that will restore it to its original condition, the fully functioning state it enjoyed when it was first created. As these repairs proceed in the restoration/renewal process and a detrimental modification to the original design is discovered, that modification must be removed. It must be removed so that it will not interfere with its operating as it was originally designed. Further, to properly renew anything, we must understand its original design. The best way to renew something is with the direction and assistance of the original builder. A builder in Paul's day was not only the builder but also the designer and architect. With the expertise and help available through the builder, full renewal is best accomplished.

If you are renewing a house, that house's builder would best know how to go about it. If you are renewing an automobile, that automobile's builder would best know how to go about it. In our case, we are renewing the mind. It stands to reason, then, that its renewal would best be accomplished in partnership with its Architect/Builder—God.

We know that it is the mind that is to be renewed, and that we should partner with God to accomplish its renewal, but what is it about the mind that is being renewed? Is it broken, in need of new parts?

When Paul says that it is the mind which is being renewed when spiritual transformation is taking place, he means much more than what most of us think of when we use the word *mind*. Most of us think of the mind as some sort of calculator in our head, so it's understandable that our idea of renewing it would start with the idea of replacing its broken parts. But for Paul, the mind is much more than a calculator in our head, and to renew it means more than simply swapping out a sticky key, or a cracked screen, or replacing the batteries that have run low.

The Greek word that Paul uses and is translated as the English word mind is νους. Here it means the inner direction of one's thoughts and will and the orientation of one's moral consciousness. When Paul refers to our mind's renewal, he is saying that the current direction of our thoughts and will must be changed. The way our mind currently directs our thoughts and will no longer leads to where the mind was originally designed to take our thoughts and will. Our mind no longer leads our thinking to know the will of God, to know what is good, pleasing, and perfect, and no longer directs our will to accomplish God's will, to do what is good, pleasing, and perfect. This is in large part what is meant by being lost. If our minds are not renewed, then we cannot live a life directed toward doing what is pleasing to God. We need to undergo the restoration process that will return our minds to operating as they were originally designed, allowing our minds to direct our thinking and will toward God. The good news is that the original Builder/Architect—God—prescribed the renewing of the mind as the sure remedy to restoring us to spiritual health, and He intends to partner with us in this restoration process.

For spiritual transformation to occur there must be a partnership between the Holy Spirit and the person who is to undergo transformation. It is good news that the Holy Spirit is involved in the process of our restoration because, unlike other things that undergo restoration, like houses, tables, and chairs, we are not just passive things. We are more. We are *beings*, *human* beings, *made* in the image of God. Being made in the image of God includes much more than I will (or even can) mention, but for our purposes it includes having thoughts, ideas, passions, desires, and a will of our own. Because these abilities in their current condition (i.e., before renewal) no longer lead us toward God's will, we do not have the ability to direct our own transformation. We need someone who is not "conformed to the pattern of this world," one who is completely conformed to the will of God, to direct the renewal. And because we are in this prerenewal condition, we need someone to initiate, to enable us, and encourage us to continue the process, someone who is not subject to the same problems our condition allows. Who is better to direct than God? Who is better to enable and encourage than God? There is none better suited to the task than the Holy Spirit. That we are partnering with Him is good news indeed!

With the initiating, enabling, and direction of the Holy Spirit, the process of renewal can begin. It is a two-stage process: the *appropriation of the truth* and the *application of truth-directed behavior*. The first stage, the *appropriation of the truth*, takes place when:

1. We have the desire to pursue the Truth to be changed;
2. We then act upon that desire, choosing to pursue the Truth by setting our will.

The second stage, the *application of truth-directed behavior*, takes place when:

1. We begin practicing behaviors, which we'll describe as spiritual disciplines, designed to halt our conformity to "the pattern of this world";
2. We engage in transformational activities, which are designed to reorient our mind and direct it toward God's will;
3. We continue to practice transformational activities to introduce and establish new patterns of thinking and behavior which conforms our mind to the mind of Christ.

The same components in the process for renewing the mind that we gleaned from the apostle Paul can also be seen in Jesus' call to anyone who would follow Him.

Jesus commanded to all who would follow Him (all disciples) to:

Come to me, all you who are weary and burdened, and I will
give you rest. Take my yoke upon you and learn from me, for I
am gentle and humble in heart, and you will find rest for your
souls. (Matthew 11:28-29)

Jesus begins with a promise, "Come . . . and I will give you rest." He
kindles a desire to follow Him. This is the first step in *the appropriation
of truth*, the *desire* to pursue the Truth. We *desire* change. Next Jesus'
command to take His yoke. This is the second step in the *appropriation
of truth*, *choosing* to pursue the truth. We set our *will* to change. At this
step, we can choose to pursue our desire for the truth and change or
ignore it. If we choose to delay placing it upon our shoulders it is at the
cost of rest to our souls. The choice precedes the action. Next, we read
that we are to take His yoke.

To take His yoke is the first step of the second stage in the process
of renewing the mind, the *application of truth-directed behavior*. At this
step, as we saw before with Paul, we discontinue with our current ways,
which conform us to the pattern of this world. We intentionally begin
to dislodge the destructive patterns that have grown in us as a precursor
to the second step, the taking-upon of a new way, God's way, His yoke.

The second step, the taking-upon of Jesus' yoke, is the part of the
process of renewing the mind where the vacancy left from dislodging
our old ways, "the pattern of this world," is being filled up with the new
life-giving patterns by which we are to conform our lives. It is this yoke,
God's new way of living the life that Jesus lived, that is to be taken upon
us. Just as the yoke for an ox is placed upon its body, allowing the power
of the ox to perform its master's work (work the ox would otherwise
not be able to accomplish), so also Jesus' yoke must be placed upon our
body to allow it to perform our Master's work, the renewing of our mind
(work we would otherwise not be able to accomplish).

Finally, we see the third, and last step, in the *application of truth-
directed behavior*. This is the final step in the process of renewal, but it is
also the beginning step in the ongoing process of our spiritual transformation. It finally brings us all the way to our taking Jesus' yoke upon us.

It also begins the continuing journey of knowing and doing God's good, pleasing, and perfect will. While the second step trains the mind through establishing patterns, the third step lives out the new character that has replaced the old. This continuing journey begins once we take His yoke upon us. For then we begin to "learn from me [Jesus]" and thereby experience rest for our soul. This rest, this peacefulness that comes from learning from Jesus, is what it is to live with a renewed mind. It is experiencing the Spirit-initiated, encouraged, enabled, and empowered life Jesus enjoyed with the peace that comes only by having the "mind of Christ" and by accomplishing His good, pleasing, and perfect will.

EXPERIENCE THE LIFE provides the disciple a structured process whereby he can engage in the process of spiritual renewal. It provides a daily regimen for practicing specific disciplines designed to displace those old destructive ideas and behaviors (the patterns of the world) and replacing them with new, constructive, life-giving ideas and behaviors (the mind of Christ).

EXPERIENCE THE LIFE requires commitment to consistently practice the disciplines and to reserve the time required for transformation.

Most studies on change agree that displacing a current habit or idea and establishing a new one requires a minimum of about three months. Also, learning studies demonstrate the necessity of consistent application of the thing being learned to ensure its permanent retention.

According to a leading learning researcher, people remember:

- 10% of what they read
- 20% of what they hear
- 30% of what they see
- 50% of what they see and hear
- 70% of what they say
- 95% of what they teach someone else[1]

---

1. William Glassner, *Control Therapy in the Classroom* (New York: Harper and Row, 1986); *Reality Therapy: A New Approach to Psychiatry* (New York: Harper and Row, 1965).

Simply put, we learn best not by passively hearing and seeing, but by actively "doing" the thing which we are learning.

The most relevant question a teacher can ask is, "Are my students learning?" For our purposes, the relevant question must be, "Am I engaged in a process that will result in my being changed from what I am into what I am to be? Am I being transformed into the image of Christ?"

Each book in this series provides a solid opportunity for significant transformation through the use of several common tools or disciplines including:

- Reading Scripture together
- Reading a common philosophy of the Christian experience
- Journaling insights, questions, and prayers
- Discussion over material that has already been studied, prayed over, and reflected upon
- Accountability for the purpose of helping each other keep their commitments to God
- Encouragement to help each other overcome areas of defeat and break free of bondage
- Mutual commitment to apply what God has impressed on each member
- Mutual commitment to impact those with whom they have contact

Its Pattern

This course leads the believer to *experience the life* Jesus lived, utilizing a daily regimen to practice the various spiritual disciplines. The course is thirty weeks long over five books.

The five books, each six weeks in length, instruct and challenge the disciples to conform their life to:

1. Believe as Jesus believed,
2. Live as Jesus lived,
3. Love as Jesus loved,

4. Minister as Jesus ministered, and

5. Lead as Jesus led.

Each six-week book leads disciples through a course of daily teachings and exercises in an examination of how Jesus lived out His faith.

In Daily Session Five, the disciple begins with a prayer focused on the issues to be presented in the daily reading. The daily reading gives a core thought that will be explored in the day's exercises. Questions are designed to help the disciple's understanding of the core thoughts and key ideas. Disciples are then directed to reflect on the application of these core thoughts and key ideas to their own spiritual growth. Journaling space is provided for answering questions and recording thoughts, questions, applications, and insights stemming from her reflection.

Once weekly (the sixth session), the disciple meets with others who comprise her community. At the community meeting they pray together, discuss the core thoughts and key ideas introduced in the week's readings, and share from their own experience of practicing the week's spiritual discipline. They view and discuss the video introduction for the following week's study and pray and encourage one another in their journey of spiritual transformation.

Although the books were designed primarily for use by groups consisting of two to six members, the material and the format can easily be used to effectively lead larger groups in a discussion-based exploration of spiritual transformation.

Lastly, we recommend that the leaders of the weekly discussion groups proceed through each book together as a community group prior to leading their own group. The insights that they will acquire from their own journey through EXPERIENCE THE LIFE will be invaluable to them and the larger group they will lead.

When leading a larger group through EXPERIENCE THE LIFE, keep in mind that most of the spiritual traction for transformation is due to the interaction that the Lord has with each individual through the other individuals in a community of believers. To preserve this traction, the leader must provide a venue and time for this interaction. For this reason, we suggest that some time during the weekly session, the leader divide the large group into smaller groups mimicking the two- to six-member community group for the purpose of more intimately discussing the issues presented in the week's session. It is reported after experiencing successive weeks with the same members of this smaller discussion group individuals previously not participants in a small-group program have desired to continue in such a program.

While we believe that the most effective and efficient means of leading individuals to healthy spiritual transformation is in the context of a smaller community group, we do acknowledge that the larger group setting may be the only means currently available to a church's leadership. Though the *form* of instruction is important, the *function* is what must be preserved: *Verum supremus vultus* (truth above form).

Its Product

Each session is designed to challenge the disciple to examine the progress of his own transformation, to train him with the desire to both know God's will and do it. This course values the spiritual traction the disciple can get by facing this challenge in a high-trust community. Christ was a Man for others. Disciples then are to be people for others. It is only in losing ourselves in the mission of loving others that we live in balance and experience the joy that Christ has promised. And therein lies many of the rewards a disciple may enjoy as he lives and loves as Jesus. This is the life that cultivates Christlikeness and whose product is a transformed disciple—the only life of faith worthy of justifying our calling upon others to EXPERIENCE THE LIFE.

WEEK 1

Being Led by God into Temptation to Deliverance

DAY ONE

Prayer

Dear Jesus, my desire is to have Your strength of character. I want to be able to do what is right even when doing so becomes difficult. I want to stand firm in my faith when it is put to the test. Please reveal to me whatever I need to do to be able to live the abundant life of obedience that You live. Amen.

Core Thought

Yes, God does lead us into temptation.

When Jesus answered the disciples' question about how they should pray, saying that they should ask the Father not to lead them into temptation, His point was not that God did not lead them into times when they would be tempted. As Jews, the disciples knew their own history well. God did lead their people into times when He tested them.

Jesus' disciples knew that Abram was tempted in the wilderness (Genesis 12:10–13:11), obeyed with the offering of Isaac (Genesis 22), and was delivered. Moses and the children of Israel were tempted in the wilderness (Exodus), and those who obeyed were delivered. David, during his exile, was tempted in the wilderness (1 Samuel 24), obeyed, and was delivered. The Father had always used the tool of temptation to reveal a child's true allegiance. They understood that those who had true faith responded to temptation with acts of obedience, that the faithful would follow only God's leading. And that those who obeyed experienced God's deliverance.

Jesus was teaching the disciples to pray that they would obediently follow the Father's leading into, through, and beyond those times of temptation so that they could experience His power to deliver them.

Through these next weeks as we study and meditate upon the temptations of Christ, we will see that God the Father uses what seems to us the most paradoxical of methods for transforming us from what we are into who we are to be. He uses temptation for transformation.

Today's Exercises

Core Scripture: Matthew 3:15-17
Read aloud Matthew 3:15-17.
Recite this week's memory verses aloud five times.

> Consider it pure joy, my brothers, whenever you face trials of many kinds, because you know that the testing of your faith develops perseverance. Perseverance must finish its work so that you may be mature and complete, not lacking anything. (James 1:2-4)

Meditate on today's passage.

Request to Be in His Presence

"Dear Lord, bring me into the context of Your world."

1. ***Read it***—Remember: We read now only what is there, to hear once again, only what was spoken then.

   Read Matthew 1:17 at least twice, out loud.
2. ***Think it***—select a portion, a phrase within the reading, mull it over in your mind, thinking about the context and setting, reimagining the event, putting yourself into the situation. As you meditate, use all five senses to re-create the context and the setting by building the images that are supplied within the passages.

3. ***Pray it***—ask God to give you understanding into how the truths He has spoken in these Scriptures apply to you now. Ask, "What is it about me that I need to deal with? What is it about me that must change?"

   Respond to God by accepting and admitting whatever responsibility is implied by what He has shown. Write what it is that God has shown you, and what you must admit responsibility for having done (or not done).

4. ***Live it***—ask God to reveal to you what He wants you to do about what you have admitted.

   List what particular action(s) you will take today to accomplish what God has revealed for you to do.

Pray, asking the Holy Spirit to empower you to act in obedience and to accomplish what He has revealed for you to do today.

Discovering the Discipline: Fasting
What Is Fasting?
"The essence of a fast is self-denial in order to direct the thoughts to God," said Charles E. Wolfe in a published sermon. "Traditionally this has been the decision not to eat food for a certain length of time so that hunger will remind us of God"[1]

---

1. Charles E. Wolfe, quoted in Lisa Master, "Uncovering Fasting," *Worldwide Challenge,* March/ April 1996, http://www.wwcmagazine.org/1996/lisafast.html (accessed July 23, 2007).

A few render a broader definition, advocating voluntarily refraining from television, people, sleep, or sexual relations.

The Purpose of Fasting

The primary purpose for practicing the spiritual discipline of fasting is to train ourselves to hear and focus on God's voice. That is why fasting must always be combined first and foremost with extended times of prayer.

Early on in this practice, the pangs of hunger can serve as reminders to focus our attention on hearing what God has to say to us. As we develop in this practice, our hearts and minds become more spiritually sensitive to God's voice and less distracted by the complaints voiced by our own bodies.

One reason for practicing spiritual disciplines is to eliminate the things that keep us from experiencing the fullness of life in God. Through this practice of abstaining from food and/or drink, God can break our bondage to being satisfied by satisfying ourselves through our bodily desires.

The more our spiritual hearing becomes attuned to God's voice and less to our own, the more in tune we will be to the voice of the Spirit of God as He leads us.

When Jesus fasted in the desert, He was tempted to turn stones into loaves of bread, but He said, "Man does not live on bread alone, but on every word that comes from the mouth of God" (Matthew 4:4). Another time, when Jesus' disciples urged Jesus to eat some food, He responded, "I have food to eat that you know nothing about. . . . My food . . . is to do the will of him who sent me and to finish his work" (John 4:32,34). In abstaining from food and/or drink, we discover an alternative source of strength, another kind of food. By abstaining from normal food we begin to develop a taste for the divine kind of food, the bread of God's own words, and the work of fulfilling God's will.

Fasting, however, will reveal more than our dependence on food. As we focus on the presence of God and hearing His voice, instead of attending to the cravings and ravings of our bodies, the content of our character will be revealed to us. We will have a heightened spiritual awareness of being in God's presence, and being in the light of the nearness of His presence will result in the revealing of the condition of our own hearts. As Richard Foster wrote, "Anger, bitterness, jealousy, strife, fear—if they are within us, they will surface during fasting."[2] This is a benefit to us because with these things revealed, they can now also be addressed, and the process of our transformation will excel.

As we continue the spiritual discipline of fasting, we will begin to prefer the Voice of the Master to the other voices (including our own) which lead us astray. It is this kind of follower that Jesus described:

> And the sheep listen to his [the Shepherd's] voice. He calls his own sheep by name and leads them out. When he has brought out all his own, he goes on ahead of them, and his sheep follow him because they know his voice. But they will never follow a stranger; in fact, they will run away from him because they do not recognize a stranger's voice. (John 10:3-5)

Doing the Discipline: Fasting
Determining the Purpose of My Fasting

This week we will begin to prepare for the first of three fasts that we will be engaging in over the course of these next six weeks of *Book Two*. This week we will prepare for the one-day, water-only fast that you will begin on Day Three of Week Two.

The first step in preparing for the one-day fast is for you to determine the purpose of your fasting (see above). To help you define the purpose of your fast, we have included some questions that you can ask yourself (and some that you can ask the Lord) designed to reveal areas where God's Spirit can expose things about your character and mission that need further definition and refinement.

---

2. Richard Foster, *Celebration of Discipline* (New York: Harper and Row, 1978), 55.

Questions

1. Does your faith feel like it has lost its power, its zeal, its zest? What other things crowd out your commitment to Christ, and your closeness to Him? Fasting and prayer can restore the loss of the first love for your Lord and result in a more intimate relationship with Christ.

2. Do you need to have things your way; do you talk too much, hope that your name will be mentioned, feel the need to be recognized for what you have done? Fasting is a biblical way to humble yourself in the sight of God (Ezra 8:21). King David said, "I humbled myself with fasting" (Psalm 35:13).

3. Has it been a while since you have taken a spiritual inventory of your faith? Fasting enables the Holy Spirit to reveal your true spiritual condition, resulting in brokenness, repentance, and a transformed life.

4. Are you no longer moved by what you hear from the Word of God? The Holy Spirit will quicken the Word of God in your heart and His truth will become more meaningful to you.

5. Is your prayer life missing, lacking, or becoming an unrewarding experience? Fasting can transform your prayer life into a richer and more personal experience.

6. Are you having less or little impact on the lives of others? Fasting can result in a dynamic personal revival in your own life and make you a channel of revival to others.[3]

7. Are you in need of direction regarding some decision in your life? Fasting will provide a focused time of seeking after God's leading and the quiet necessary to hear and recognize his voice. Fasting even renders clarity of mind. Fasting "imparts a degree of acuteness to the understanding," said Samuel Miller, "of vigor to the imagination, and of activity and promptness to the memory, which are not experienced in other circumstances."[4]

---

3. Bill Bright, "Your Personal Guide to Fasting and Prayer," Campus Crusade for Christ, http://www.billbright.com/howtofast/ (accessed July 23, 2007).

4. Samuel Miller quoted in Lisa Master, "Uncovering Fasting," http://www.wwcmagazine .org/1996/lisafast.html, 2007.

Journal

Record ideas, impressions, feelings, questions, and any insights you may have had during today's time.

Prayer

Pray for each member of your community.

Being Led by God into Temptation to Deliverance

DAY TWO

Prayer

Dear Lord, I've become accustomed to having what I want when I want it so I don't feel very tempted about things. I'm not in the habit of denying myself anything. However, I have noticed that I'm not very happy when things aren't going my way. I can feel and make others feel pretty miserable at times. I am not proud of being like this. I'd like You to help me change. Help me to grow and become someone who can be contented and joyful even when the world is not treating me right. Amen.

Core Thought

> God leads us into temptation; He always has.

To understand the meaning of the temptation of Christ, we must start by understanding the stories that immediately precede His temptation by Satan. Just as the genealogy of Christ was used to remind us of the temptation, obedience, and deliverance of Abraham, Moses and the children of Israel, and David, so these stories that precede the temptation of Christ serve to show that God has always accomplished His will by leading the faithful into temptation.

Before Jesus is tested by the Devil, we are told of the tempting of Joseph, Mary, the Magi, and John the Baptist. When Joseph learns that his betrothed is pregnant, he is tempted to "put her away quietly" to avoid the public disgrace (see Matthew 1:19). Mary is tempted to doubt God's word when she learns that she will become pregnant as a virgin

(Luke 1:34-38). The Magi are tempted when compelled by Herod to disclose the whereabouts of the newborn King of Israel (Matthew 2:8). John the Baptist is tempted to enjoy the normal comforts and attire of the day, the approval of the religious professionals, and the good graces of the king (Mark 1:4-7; Luke 7:24-25; Matthew 3:7-10; Mark 6:17-19).

In each of these accounts we see God leading His people into their own times of temptation. We also see each responding by being obedient to God's leading despite whatever consequences should come. And as a result, in each case we see God revealing Himself and His plan to them, showing them what part they are to play in it.

Tomorrow, we will study and meditate on how God used temptation to produce in these people the character that they so admirably demonstrated.

Today's Exercises

Core Scripture: Matthew 3:15-17
Read aloud Matthew 3:15-17.
Recite this week's memory verses aloud five times.

> Consider it pure joy, my brothers, whenever you face trials of many kinds, because you know that the testing of your faith develops perseverance. Perseverance must finish its work so that you may be mature and complete, not lacking anything. (James 1:2-4)

Meditate on today's passage.

Request to Be in His Presence
"Dear Lord, bring me into the context of Your world."

1. *Read it*—Remember: We read now only what is there, to hear once again, only what was spoken then.
   Read Matthew 1:18 at least twice, out loud.
2. *Think it*—select a portion, a phrase within the reading, mull it over in your mind, thinking about the context and setting,

reimagining the event, putting yourself into the situation. As you meditate, use all five senses to re-create the context and the setting by building the images that are supplied within the passages.

3. *Pray it*—ask God to give you understanding into how the truths He has spoken in these Scriptures apply to you now. Ask, "What is it about me that I need to deal with? What is it about me that must change?"

    Respond to God by accepting and admitting whatever responsibility is implied by what He has shown. Write what it is that God has shown you, and what you must admit responsibility for having done (or not done).

4. *Live it*—ask God to reveal to you what He wants you to do about what you have admitted.

List what particular action(s) you will take today to accomplish what God has revealed for you to do.

Pray, asking the Holy Spirit to empower you to act in obedience and to accomplish what He has revealed for you to do today.

Discovering the Discipline: Fasting

The Privation of Fasting

One reason for practicing spiritual disciplines is to eliminate the things that keep us from experiencing the fullness of life in God. Through the practice of fasting, abstaining from food and/or drink, God can break our bondage to satisfying ourselves through our bodily desires.

The more our spiritual hearing becomes attuned to God's voice and less to our own, the more in tune we will be to the voice of the

Spirit of God as He leads us.

When Jesus fasted in the desert He was tempted to turn stones into loaves of bread, but He said, "Man does not live on bread alone, but on every word that comes from the mouth of God" (Matthew 4:4). Another time, when Jesus' disciples urged Jesus to eat some food, He responded, "I have food to eat that you know nothing about. . . . My food is to do the will of him who sent me and to finish his work" (John 4:32,34). In abstaining from food and/or drink, we discover an alternative source of strength, another kind of food. By abstaining from normal food we begin to develop a taste for the divine kind of food, the bread of God's own words and doing the work of fulfilling God's will.

Doing the Discipline: Fasting

Determining the Privation of My Fasting and Dedicating My Physical Self as a Sacrifice to God

The second step in preparing for the one-day fast is for you to determine the *privation* of your fasting, that which you will *deprive* yourself of during your fast. Of course, as you are learning the discipline of fasting, we have chosen the privation for this fast (i.e., privation of all foods). In the next fast, you will learn how to align the privation of your fast with the purpose God has revealed for your fasting. For now, we will focus on the crucial step that changes fasting from merely another kind of diet to a powerful tool used by God to transform us.

Fasting is only dieting if we dedicate ourselves merely to abstaining from eating food because it is good for us. As wise as it may be for us to at times dedicate ourselves to dieting for our physical health's sake, successful diet will not bring about the type of changes God intends for us through fasting. Fasting is a powerful tool in God's hand when those who fast have dedicated their bodies as "living sacrifices" to be used by God to accomplish His will, His way. Fasting teaches us never to be a slave to our own desire by developing the habit of ignoring our desires and developing the habit of preferring God's desire, "his good pleasing and perfect will" (Romans 12:1-2).

Journal

Record ideas, impressions, feelings, questions, and any insights you may have had during today's time.

Prayer

Pray for each member of your community.

Being Led by God into Temptation to Deliverance

DAY THREE

Prayer

Dear Lord, I don't want to live out my life regretting that I have never been the kind of Christian that enjoys a personal friendship with You. I want my times of prayer to be times of conversation and joy knowing that You enjoy spending time with me. Amen.

Core Thought

> God leads us into temptation; He always will, because it is there where we will personally experience the power of God.

When we ask the question, "What do I have to do to have the godly character I see in the likes of Joseph and Mary, the Magi, and John the Baptist?" and then recount their stories, the answer becomes plain. For anyone to acquire godly character it must be formed in them, and temptation is the principal means by which our current character has been formed and is transformed into godly character.

Our character is formed by how we act in response to the many things that present themselves to our attention. Temptation occurs when our attention is presented with something that promises to satisfy us in some way while our current character objects to our being satisfied in the way that is being proposed. This being so, what we have to do to have godly character is to correctly respond to temptation. And of course herein lies the rub. To have godly character means that godlike actions flow out of us naturally, that they flow from our Godlike nature.

And that is precisely the nature we do not have. The actions that flow out of us naturally are everything but godly. It is here where God steps in and presents us with the solution that could come from nowhere else. Paradoxically, God will use temptation to transform our current character into godly character by working His own godly actions through us to develop godly desires for us to enjoy. When we examine how God uses temptation to form us, we can see that it is a perfect tool in His hands, and His purpose is to greatly benefit us.

First, in God's hands, temptation benefits us by exposing the current state of our character, our areas of weakness. From this we can learn what we are using and relying upon to get what we want, what we are using in place of God's power, and what we are desiring instead of God's will. Temptation also exposes the extent to which we desire these other things more than God. Through God's use of temptation we are made completely conscious of our weaknesses. It is only with this awareness that we can confess their sinfulness, renounce our preference for them, and begin to cooperate with God to change us.

Second, as we cooperate with God in the midst of temptation, we develop our spiritual muscles of dependence. Yes, more paradox. In our workaday world, when temptations present themselves they provide us with opportunities to train ourselves to become less dependent on our own strengths and more on His power. By this process of becoming weak in ourselves, we develop our strength in Him to endure.

And finally, in God's hand temptation is the tool He most often uses to allow us to experience His presence and understand His calling for our lives. Through enduring temptation we, like Joseph and Mary, the Magi, and the Baptist, experience what living is like when the Father is leading us from within us. For us, experiencing God as He works from inside us to affect the world outside of us is the most intimate way of knowing Him. Tomorrow, we will explore how God uses temptation to reveal Himself to the world outside of us.

Today's Exercises

Core Scripture: Matthew 3:15-17

Read aloud Matthew 3:15-17.

Recite this week's memory verses aloud five times.

> Consider it pure joy, my brothers, whenever you face trials of many kinds, because you know that the testing of your faith develops perseverance. Perseverance must finish its work so that you may be mature and complete, not lacking anything. (James 1:2-4)

Meditate on today's passage.

Request to Be in His Presence

"Dear Lord, bring me into the context of Your world."

1. *Read it*—Remember: We read now only what is there, to hear once again, only what was spoken then.

    Read Matthew 1:19-25 at least twice, out loud.

2. *Think it*—select a portion, a phrase within the reading, mull it over in your mind, thinking about the context and setting, reimagining the event, putting yourself into the situation. As you meditate, use all five senses to re-create the context and the setting by building the images that are supplied within the passages.

3. *Pray it*—ask God to give you understanding into how the truths He has spoken in these Scriptures apply to you now. Ask, "What is it about me that I need to deal with? What is it about me that must change?"

    Respond to God by accepting and admitting whatever responsibility is implied by what He has shown. Write what it is that God has shown you, and what you must admit responsibility for having done (or not done).

4. *Live it*—ask God to reveal to you what He wants you to do about what you have admitted.

List what particular action(s) you will take today to accomplish what God has revealed for you to do.

Pray, asking the Holy Spirit to empower you to act in obedience and to accomplish what He has revealed for you to do today.

Discovering the Discipline: Fasting
The Period of Fasting

The discipline of fasting will do much more than simply reveal our dependence on food, but it will not even do that if care is not taken in determining the period and duration. The period of any fast should be of sufficient length that the full gamut of uncomfortable feelings associated with our being hungry will be experienced. As with any training, this spiritual workout will be ineffective in revealing or changing anything about us if it does not cause us to raise a sweat.

This training to be able to stay focused on the presence of God and to hear His voice instead of attending to the cravings and ravings of our bodies will challenge and serve to reveal the content of our character. If the period of our fasting is sufficient, it will allow for our having a heightened spiritual awareness of being in God's presence, and being in the light of the nearness of His presence will always result in revealing the condition of our own hearts. As Richard Foster wrote, "Anger, bitterness, jealousy, strife, fear, if they are within us, they will surface during fasting."[1] This is a benefit to us because with these things revealed, they can now also be addressed, and the process of our transformation will excel.

---

1. Foster, *Celebration*, 55.

Doing the Discipline: Fasting

Determining the Period of My Fasting

The third step in preparing for the one-day fast is for you to determine the *period* of your fasting, the duration of your fast. Of course, as you are learning the discipline of fasting, we have chosen the period for this fast (one day). In the next fast, we will learn how to align the period or duration of your fast with the purpose God has revealed for your fasting. For now, we will focus on another crucial step that makes fasting a powerful tool used by God to transform us.

Yesterday we learned that we must dedicate our physical body as a living sacrifice for God to use in accomplishing His will. Today we will learn that we must direct our spirit's passion toward desiring God.

What we are doing when we direct our spirit's passion toward God is taking all the aspirations we have for ourselves, all the goals we desire to accomplish, and all the recognition we would like to receive, and putting them on hold. We give them to God, believing that whatever we found desirable in those things will be given to us at the right time in the right way. Once we have done this, we are free to focus on making the accomplishing of His will our only passion.

To live as Jesus lived we must dedicate our body and direct our spirit's passion to God. This is what is meant by loving the Lord "with all your heart, soul, mind, and strength" (Mark 12:30).

Journal

Record ideas, impressions, feelings, questions, and any insights you may have had during today's time.

Prayer

Pray for each member of your community.

Being Led by God into Temptation to Deliverance

DAY FOUR

Prayer

Dear Lord, for as long as I can remember, I have resisted being in places and doing things that would unmistakably identify me as a Christian. I don't wear religious logos on my clothes or apply bumper stickers to my car. Don't get me wrong, Lord, I would never deny that I'm a Christian if someone were to ask. I'm just not comfortable advertising. Yet, as strange as it sounds, I've always wanted to be someone who would draw people to You. I wouldn't mind if the word got out. I would like to be someone You use to love others into the family. Lord, please lead the way; I want to follow. Amen.

Core Thought

> God leads us into temptation because we are how others can personally witness the power of His presence and experience the deliverance of His saving love.

Most people can usually spot a phony a mile away and a religious phony at five miles. How? Phonies never do all that it takes to be whoever it is they are impersonating. They never pay the full price it costs to be the genuine article. If they did they would not be phonies. Those who seek truth (this would exclude those who are uninterested or resignedly cynical—they are not interested in what is true) will believe what someone says to be true if their lives (their actions) lend credibility to their claim.

God uses the tempting of believers to reveal Himself to those who have not yet trusted Him to save them. Our actions will always speak louder about what we believe than will our mere words. So, nothing will speak as loudly and will ring truer to the people who know us but do not yet believe in Jesus than what they see us doing in response to the temptations through which God is leading us.

When a believer responds to temptation with obedience, those who do not yet believe can witness the power of God's presence sustaining the believer through their times of suffering. They can see how God blesses those who obediently follow after Him. For the unbeliever, this supplies the prerequisite of faith, believing "that he exists and that he rewards those who earnestly seek him" (Hebrews 11:6).

Today's Exercises
Core Scripture: Matthew 3:15-17
Read aloud Matthew 3:15-17.
Recite this week's memory verses aloud five times.

> Consider it pure joy, my brothers, whenever you face trials of many kinds, because you know that the testing of your faith develops perseverance. Perseverance must finish its work so that you may be mature and complete, not lacking anything. (James 1:2-4)

Meditate on today's passage.

Request to Be in His Presence
"Dear Lord, bring me into the context of Your world."

1. **Read it**—Remember: We read now only what is there, to hear once again, only what was spoken then.
   Read Matthew 2:1-12 at least twice, out loud.
2. **Think it**—select a portion, a phrase within the reading, mull it over in your mind, thinking about the context and setting, reimagining the event, putting yourself into the situation. As you meditate, use all five senses to re-create the context and

the setting by building the images that are supplied within the passages.

3. *Pray it*—ask God to give you understanding into how the truths He has spoken in these Scriptures apply to you now. Ask, "What is it about me that I need to deal with? What is it about me that must change?"

   Respond to God by accepting and admitting whatever responsibility is implied by what He has shown. Write what it is that God has shown you, and what you must admit responsibility for having done (or not done).

4. *Live it*—ask God to reveal to you what He wants you to do about what you have admitted.

List what particular action(s) you will take today to accomplish what God has revealed for you to do.

Pray, asking the Holy Spirit to empower you to act in obedience and to accomplish what He has revealed for you to do today.

Discovering the Discipline: Fasting
The Perspective of Fasting

As we continue to practice the spiritual discipline of fasting, we will begin to prefer the Voice of the Master to the other voices (including our own) that lead us astray. It is this kind of follower that Jesus described when He said:

And the sheep listen to his [the Shepherd's] voice. He calls his own sheep by name and leads them out. When he has brought out all his own, he goes on ahead of them, and his sheep follow him because they know his voice. But they will never follow a stranger; in fact, they will run away from him because they do not recognize a stranger's voice. (John 10:3-5)

Doing the Discipline: Fasting
Documenting My Perspective During My Fasting

It is important to document what you experience during your fast. Keep a running narrative (some call this journaling) of your thoughts, ideas, questions, emotions, and bodily feelings throughout your time of fasting. This journal will be used at the conclusion of your fast. It is another tool to help you understand what God is teaching you, why you need this teaching, and how He intends for you to use what He is teaching you to accomplish His will, His way.

Journal

Record ideas, impressions, feelings, questions, and any insights you may have had during today's time.

Prayer

Pray for each member of your community.

Being Led by God into Temptation to Deliverance

DAY FIVE

Prayer

Dear Lord, if what is required for You to transform my character to make it like Yours is that I have to go through painful and unpleasant circumstances, then all I have to say is . . . that really scares me. I like the idea of being like You. I just don't like the idea that suffering is what it's going to take. So, if it is, help me, and go easy! I don't trust myself to keep at it. Help me not to jump ship on you. Amen.

Core Thought

> To live as Jesus lived, we must train ourselves to follow God into temptation, because in God's skillful hands even temptation is transformational.

As we discovered earlier this week, God does lead us into temptation. He uses temptation to form in us the ability to respond naturally to temptation with godlike actions. This is paradoxical, especially given that the actions we naturally display show that we are anything but godlike. His use of temptation to transform us can only be accomplished by God Himself living out His own godly actions through us as He lives in us. Through enduring the suffering that comes with temptation, we experience intimacy with God and enjoy the power of His deliverance. Also, our response to suffering through temptation provides the opportunity for unbelievers to witness God being present and acting, giving credible reasons for them to believe "that he exists and that he rewards those who earnestly seek him" (Hebrews 11:6).

Temptation can be transformational only because it is caused to be so by our Father who "causes all things to work together for good to those who love God, to those who are called according to His purpose" (Romans 8:28, NASB). It is transformational only because He is both governing its use and enabling us to respond correctly to its challenge.

Lastly, temptation can be transformational only if there is a willingness to follow God as He leads us into and through temptation. We will begin that exploration next week.

Today's Exercises

Core Scripture: Matthew 3:15-17
Read aloud Matthew 3:15-17.
Recite this week's memory verses aloud five times.

> Consider it pure joy, my brothers, whenever you face trials of many
> kinds, because you know that the testing of your faith develops
> perseverance. Perseverance must finish its work so that you may
> be mature and complete, not lacking anything. (James 1:2-4)

Meditate on today's passage.

Request to Be in His Presence

"Dear Lord, bring me into the context of Your world."

1. **Read it**—Remember: We read now only what is there, to hear once again, only what was spoken then.
   Read Matthew 3:1-4,11-14 at least twice, out loud.
2. **Think it**—select a portion, a phrase within the reading, mull it over in your mind, thinking about the context and setting, reimagining the event, putting yourself into the situation. As you meditate, use all five senses to re-create the context and the setting by building the images that are supplied within the passages.

3. *Pray it*—ask God to give you understanding into how the truths He has spoken in these Scriptures apply to you now. Ask, "What is it about me that I need to deal with? What is it about me that must change?"

Respond to God by accepting and admitting whatever responsibility is implied by what He has shown. Write what it is that God has shown you, and what you must admit responsibility for having done (or not done).

4. *Live it*—ask God to reveal to you what He wants you to do about what you have admitted.

List what particular action(s) you will take today to accomplish what God has revealed for you to do.

Pray, asking the Holy Spirit to empower you to act in obedience and to accomplish what He has revealed for you to do today.

Discovering the Discipline: Fasting

The Profit of Fasting

When we talk about what profit or benefit we received from our having fasted, we must tread carefully. While it is true that personally we will receive the benefits of having fasted, the real profit is shared. We will never reap the true benefits of fasting so long as we value it only for the benefits it brings to us individually. Of course, the first benefits of fasting are experienced by the individual.

Fasting should be valued at first for its medicinal property. When we begin to practice the discipline of fasting we must value it as a remedy. Fasting is submitting ourselves before the Great Physician to have our illness properly diagnosed and begin treatment. Initially, we engage in treatment only to rid ourselves of the discomfort or disability we are experiencing. We want to treat the symptoms. And, usually once we start feeling better, our symptoms become tolerable to us, and we stop treatment. Oftentimes we will discontinue taking the medicine the physician prescribed because we believe ourselves to be getting better. If the real goal of medical treatment was to make one's symptoms tolerable, we would be justified in stopping our meds. However, the goal of taking medicine is to eliminate whatever is keeping us from being able to enjoy a physically active life—physical health. And like it, the goal of practicing spiritual disciplines in general, and fasting in this case, is to eliminate whatever is keeping us from being able to enjoy a spiritually active life—spiritual health. But fasting brings the benefits of spiritual health not only to us; it spreads its benefits to others through us.

Thomas Ryan makes this observation:

> If fasting is doing its work of liberating our focus from self-preoccupation, this will manifest itself in mercy and compassion toward those around us. We will be moved from within to give what we are receiving from God. . . . Our lives will be marked by concrete caring responses for others. Fasting must deal with reality. It does not skirt issues. It is not an interior escape.[1]

Doing the Discipline: Fasting
Deriving the Profit from My Fasting

For fasting to be transformational it must be practiced—you have to do it. Afterward we must ask and receive answers to these questions:

1. What did I experience?
2. What do I know now, resulting from these experiences?
3. What does the Lord want me to learn from these experiences?
4. What does the Lord want me to do with what I now know?

For fasting to be transformational in my life and my life to be used

---

1. Thomas Ryan, *Fasting Rediscovered* (New York: Paulist Press, 1981), 119.

by the Holy Spirit to benefit others in their being transformed, I must derive its profit. To live as Jesus lived is to derive the personal benefits of fasting, and then spend them by acting to benefit others.

Journal

Record ideas, impressions, feelings, questions, and any insights you may have had during today's time.

Prayer

Pray for each member of your community.

Being Led by God into
Temptation to Deliverance

DAY SIX

Community Meeting

In preparation for this week's meeting, you will have read and reflected upon each of the week's five Core Thoughts, recorded your thoughts and observations, and are ready to recite this week's memory verses to the group.

WEEK 2

Being Led by God Through Temptation to Transformation

DAY ONE

Prayer

Dear Lord, please guide me in this process of transformation. I don't particularly like the idea of being led anywhere, especially somewhere that I'm likely to be uncomfortable. What I mean to say is that I don't like being expected to follow someone. I will need Your help to change. Amen.

Core Thought

> For temptation to be transformational
> its subject must be a willing servant.

Last week we saw that God uses the tempting of believers to accomplish His transforming work in them and to reveal Himself to others through them. He has used it in times past, and He continues to do so.

This week we will look in-depth at the verses that recount the temptation of Christ. By doing so, we hope to learn from His example what we must do to make the times when we are tempted occasions of personal transformation.

Matthew introduces the temptation by setting the scene, introducing the components out of which our imagination can reconstruct its occurrence. These components are the necessary conditions that must exist for any temptation to be transformational. Lacking any one of them causes there to be no temptation at all or causes the temptation to be deformational, a temptation which deforms and damages us, rather than transformational, which reforms and repairs us.

For there to be temptation at all, there must of course be a subject, a person to be tempted. But for temptation to be transformational, the person must also be a willing servant. And this is how Jesus is described:

> Then Jesus was led by the Spirit into the desert to be tempted by the devil. After fasting forty days and forty nights, he was hungry. (Matthew 4:1-2)

The very order Matthew uses indicates Jesus' willingness to serve. "Then Jesus was led," says Matthew. (Mark writes, "At once, the Spirit sent him.") The idea is that first, the Spirit of God told Jesus to go, and the very next thing that happened was that Jesus obeyed and went (Mark 1:12). The order of Jesus' actions demonstrates the priorities upon which His (and any willing servant's) actions must be based. First, Jesus hears and obeys—He follows the Spirit's leading. He does this first, and He does it without questioning or preparation. He understands the situation, that He is leaving behind the comforts He enjoyed in Nazareth and the affirmation He received in Transjordan to subject Himself willingly to suffering while being tempted at the Devil's hand. It is only after He has obeyed the Spirit's leading, while He continues His obedience, that He seeks after God for further understanding and further direction, "fasting forty days and forty nights."

Matthew concludes his description by saying that at the end of Jesus' forty-day fast "he was hungry." This amazing understatement is included to lead us to think, "Well, it looks like You've gotten yourself into a fine mess now! Why didn't You take time to plan ahead, to pack some food and water? Now You're starved, too weak to do anything about it. What were You thinking? And now, look who You are up against! You really should be more self-sufficient!" The last essential quality we see in a willing servant is that he is committed to being utterly dependent upon God to sustain him while he obeys, after he has obeyed God's command, as he is following God's leading, while he is seeking God's presence and wisdom, and when he is tempted.

From Matthew's description of Jesus, we see that a willing servant is one who first hears God's voice and immediately obeys and then, while continuing to obey, begins to actively seek after God for further understanding and direction, all the while remaining utterly dependent upon God alone to sustain and enable him to accomplish His will. To live as Jesus lived is to be a willing servant.

Today's Exercises

Core Scripture: Matthew 4:1-2
Read aloud Matthew 4:1-2.
Recite this week's memory verse aloud five times.

> No temptation has seized you except what is common to man. And God is faithful; he will not let you be tempted beyond what you can bear. But when you are tempted, he will also provide a way out so that you can stand up under it. (1 Corinthians 10:13)

Meditate on today's passage.

Request to Be in His Presence

"Dear Lord, bring me into the context of Your world."

1. *Read it*—Remember: We read now only what is there, to hear once again, only what was spoken then.
   Read Matthew 4:1-2 at least twice, out loud.
2. *Think it*—select a portion, a phrase within the reading, mull it over in your mind, thinking about the context and setting, reimagining the event, putting yourself into the situation. As you meditate, use all five senses to re-create the context and the setting by building the images that are supplied within the passages.
3. *Pray it*—ask God to give you understanding into how the truths

He has spoken in these Scriptures apply to you now. Ask, "What is it about me that I need to deal with? What is it about me that must change?"

Respond to God by accepting and admitting whatever responsibility is implied by what He has shown. Write what it is that God has shown you, and what you must admit responsibility for having done (or not done).

4. *Live it*—ask God to reveal to you what He wants you to do about what you have admitted.

List what particular action(s) you will take today to accomplish what God has revealed for you to do.

Pray, asking the Holy Spirit to empower you to act in obedience and to accomplish what He has revealed for you to do today.

Discovering the Discipline: Fasting
How to Fast Safely
Consider Bill Bright's wise counsel regarding fasting:

> As you begin your fast, you may hear from concerned loved ones and friends who urge you to protect your health. And they are right. You should protect your health. But be assured, if done properly, fasting will not only prove to be a spiritual blessing, but physical blessing as well.
>
> Since our spirit and bodies are interconnected, the benefits go beyond the spiritual realm. Weight loss, cleansing our

bodies of toxins, and a sense of physical well-being come from giving our body a temporary vacation from digestion.

"Fasting is a natural physiological process," said nutritionist Dr. Julio C. Ruibal "From both the scriptural and the scientific point of view, we can have confidence that fasting is not harmful, but rather beneficial when properly carried out."

Fasting even renders clarity of mind. "[Fasting] imparts a degree of acuteness to the understanding," said Samuel Miller in *Fasting*, "of vigor to the imagination, and of activity and promptness to the memory, which are not experienced in other circumstances."

If you have questions regarding your fitness to fast, then by all means, consult your doctor before you begin your fast. But be aware that many doctors have not been trained in this area and so their understanding is limited. Even so, if you question your fitness, it would be wise to ask your doctor for a physical exam to make sure you are in good health. You may have a physical problem that would make fasting unwise or dangerous. Also, if you are under any type of medication, make sure you talk to your doctor *before* changing your regimen. Prudence and caution are in order.

In spite of the safety and benefits of fasting, there are certain persons who should *never* fast without professional supervision. For example:

- Persons who are physically too thin or emaciated
- Persons who are prone to anorexia, bulimia, or other behavioral disorders
- Those who suffer weakness or anemia
- Persons who have tumors, bleeding ulcers, cancer, blood diseases, or who have heart disease
- Those who suffer chronic problems with kidneys, liver, lungs, heart, or other important organs
- Individuals who take insulin for diabetes, or suffer any other blood sugar problem such as hyperglycemia

- Women who are pregnant or nursing[1]

If you are assured that you are in good health and fit-to-fast, then you are ready to begin preparing to fast.

Doing the Discipline: Preparing for the One-Day Fast
Determining the Purpose of My Fast

This week we will begin to prepare for the first of three fasts that we will be engaging in over the course of these next five weeks of *Book Two*. This week we will prepare for the one-day, water-only fast that will begin the evening of Day Three of this week.

The first step in preparing for the one-day fast is for you to determine the purpose of your fasting (as was described in Week One).

1. Pray that God will direct you in determining the purpose, what issue you are seeking God's directing about.
2. Review the questions we provided to help you determine the spiritual area in your life you will be focusing on during the one-day fast.
3. Write a paragraph describing the issues you will be addressing in your fast and the outcome you desire (in the space below).

The purpose of my fast, the issue upon which I will focus, and about which I will ask God's direction is:

---

1. Thomas Ryan, *Fasting Rediscovered* (New York: Paulist Press, 1981), 119.

Journal

Record ideas, impressions, feelings, questions, and any insights you may have had during today's time.

Prayer

Pray for each member of your community.

Being Led by God Through Temptation to Transformation

DAY TWO

Prayer

Dear Lord, I like the idea of being changed into being like You, of being able to think and do as You do. This really does appeal to me. I would like to wake up tomorrow and to somehow—maybe by a miracle—find myself changed, able to be and do as You. So, while I desire to be changed, I know I don't really want to have to do what it takes to become changed. Lord, please make Your presence known to me in ways that will make me so desire You that I will do anything to remain in Your presence. Amen.

Core Thought

> For temptation to be transformational it must occur under circumstances where obedience is not easy.

In our daily lives, any real temptation will present itself to us when the circumstances are more apt for us to fail than to succeed. And for temptation to be transformational the circumstances must make it such that being obedient is not easier than being disobedient.

When we look at the circumstances in which the temptation of Jesus occurs, we see a willing Servant being led by the Spirit into circumstances that appear to set Him up to fail. Just before Jesus is sent into the wilderness to be tempted, He was honored at His baptism. The Spirit of God descended on Him and the Father announced that He is His beloved Son, and that He is fully pleased with Him. Jesus was at an all-time high point in His life. From this high point, this celebration, God led Him to what in comparison must be considered a very low point, His being tempted by the Devil. To see Jesus' temptation as a low point is to recognize the emotional fall He must have experienced, from the height of celebration to depths of suffering the temptation. Yet, it was precisely from the high to the low that the Spirit of God led Him. It would seem that anyone who causes someone to experience an emotional fall of such magnitude and then immediately sends him out to accomplish something at which no one else has been successful is setting him up to fail. The Father setting up His beloved Son to fail certainly isn't what we expect from a loving father. So we should ask whether we can look at it differently. Perhaps our whole perspective is wrong.

When we consider the circumstances from the perspective of a Father who is completely confident in His Son's future performance based upon His history of being perfectly obedient, the temptation of Jesus resembles less a low point in Jesus' life and more a high point. Christ's temptation by the Devil follows the Father's confident proclamation that His beloved Son is fully able to take on any challenger and all challenges: "This is my Son, whom I love; with him I am well pleased" (Matthew 3:17). If it is a setup, it is not the Son who has been set up. This makes the circumstances of the temptation not a setup for the Son to fail, but the first great venue to display the Son's certain victory.

Temptation is transformational when it uses our circumstances as the training and proving grounds for growing our faith. To live as Jesus lived is to endure the circumstances of our temptations, knowing that they are venues for displaying Christ's faithfulness as He lives out His life in us. It is a setup for victory.

Today's Exercises

Core Scripture: Matthew 4:1-2
Read aloud Matthew 4:1-2.
Recite this week's memory verse aloud five times.

No temptation has seized you except what is common to man. And God is faithful; he will not let you be tempted

beyond what you can bear. But when you are tempted, he
will also provide a way out so that you can stand up under it.
(1 Corinthians 10:13)

Meditate on today's passage.

Request to Be in His Presence
"Dear Lord, bring me into the context of Your world."

1. ***Read it***—Remember: We read now only what is there, to hear
   once again, only what was spoken then.
      Read Matthew 4:1-2 (yes, again) at least twice, out loud.
2. ***Think it***—select a (different) portion from within the reading
   and mull it over in your mind, thinking about the context and
   setting, reimagining the event, putting yourself into the situation.
   As you meditate, use all five senses to re-create the context and
   the setting by building the images that are supplied within the
   passages.
3. ***Pray it***—ask God to give you understanding into how the truths
   He has spoken in these Scriptures apply to you now. Ask, "What
   is it about me that I need to deal with? What is it about me that
   must change?"
      Respond to God by accepting and admitting whatever
   responsibility is implied by what He has shown. Write what it is
   that God has shown you, and what you must admit responsibility
   for having done (or not done).
4. ***Live it***—ask God to reveal to you what He wants you to do
   about what you have admitted.

List what particular action(s) you will take today to accomplish what God has revealed for you to do.

Pray, asking the Holy Spirit to empower you to act in obedience and to accomplish what He has revealed for you to do today.

Doing the Discipline: Preparing for the One-Day Fast
Determining the Privation of My Fast and Dedicating My Physical Self to God

The second step in preparing for the one-day fast has two parts. In part one, you will determine the *privation* of your fasting, what it is in which you will de-*prive* yourself during your fast. Of course, as you are learning the discipline of fasting, we have chosen the privation for this fast (i.e., privation of all foods). In the next fast, you will align the privation of your fast with the purpose God has revealed for your fasting. For now we will proceed to the second part, where you will dedicate your physical self, your body and its feelings and actions, as a living sacrifice to God.

Keeping your purpose in mind, write a prayer dedicating your body, its strength, health, and comfort, as a sacrifice to God. Acknowledge that He is the one who provides for your body, and state what it is that He provides for it. Tell Him why you are giving Him this time of fasting and that you give it freely whether your purpose is fulfilled or not, that what you desire more than the fulfilling of your purpose is to enjoy this time in His presence.

My prayer of dedication to You, Lord:

Journal

Record ideas, impressions, feelings, questions, and any insights you may have had during today's time.

Prayer

Pray for each member of your community.

Being Led by God Through Temptation to Transformation

DAY THREE

Prayer

Dear Father, I've always thought that the best way to be good was to avoid the things that could make me bad. My way for becoming a better person has always been to avoid temptations. So you can see that it is quite different for me to alter my thinking to accept that You are going to make me more like Jesus by leading me to the things that I've been trying to avoid. Please help me to understand Your way. I realize that my way hasn't really worked. Amen.

Core Thought

> For temptation to be transformational
> the temptation must be real.

Matthew concludes his introduction to Christ's temptation by saying that at the end of Jesus' forty-day fast "he was hungry." The proper response to this is, "No kidding. Of course He was hungry, anyone would be hungry after not eating for forty days. I've felt like I was going to die of starvation after missing just a couple of meals!" And this is exactly the point. Matthew is showing that no matter how long it takes for you to feel really hungry, once you are you feel it just as strongly as someone for whom it takes longer to feel really hungry. You don't need to be fasting forty days nor be in the wilderness for the hunger to be real. But you do need the hunger to be real for it to be used to tempt you. Simply, the hunger that Jesus felt is the same that we feel. The sadness He felt is the same. His feeling angry, delighted, and hurt is the same as ours. It is not a sin to have these feelings. It is not even temptation to have these feelings. But it is impossible to be tempted without having these kinds of feelings.

Temptation can only occur when our feelings demand that we act to satisfy the needs to which they call attention. Experiencing the demands of our feelings is not sin, and it is not yet temptation. Temptation occurs when we begin to consider the demands our feelings are making and the actions we can use to meet their demands. This is temptation, but it is not sin. Temptation only becomes sinful once we have chosen to meet the demands of our feelings when they should not be addressed or we meet them in ways that we should not. We must remember that temptation is not sinful, nor is it sinful to be tempted. It is only sinful to respond to temptation by acting sinfully.

To live as Jesus lived is to experience the great variety and the full range of human feelings and emotions and to respond to them at the proper time in the right ways when they are used to tempt us.

Today's Exercises
Core Scripture: Matthew 4:1-2
Read aloud Matthew 4:1-2.
Recite this week's memory verse aloud five times.

> No temptation has seized you except what is common to man. And God is faithful; he will not let you be tempted beyond what you can bear. But when you are tempted, he will also provide a way out so that you can stand up under it. (1 Corinthians 10:13)

Meditate on today's passage.

Request to Be in His Presence
"Dear Lord, bring me into the context of Your world."

1. ***Read it***—Remember: We read now only what is there, to hear once again, only what was spoken then.

   Read Matthew 4:1-2 (again) at least twice, out loud.

2. ***Think it***—select a different portion, a different phrase within the reading, and mull it over in your mind, thinking about the context and setting, reimagining the event, putting yourself into the situation. As you meditate, use all five senses to re-create the context and the setting by building the images that are supplied within the passages.

3. ***Pray it***—ask God to give you understanding into how the truths He has spoken in these Scriptures apply to you now. Ask, "What is it about me that I need to deal with? What is it about me that must change?"

   Respond to God by accepting and admitting whatever responsibility is implied by what He has shown. Write what it is that God has shown you, and what you must admit responsibility for having done (or not done).

4. ***Live it***—ask God to reveal to you what He wants you to do about what you have admitted.

List what particular action(s) you will take today to accomplish what God has revealed for you to do.

Pray, asking the Holy Spirit to empower you to act in obedience and to accomplish what He has revealed for you to do today.

Doing the Discipline: Fasting
Directing My Spirit's Passions Toward God
Today you will initiate the one-day fast by beginning to direct your spirit's passion toward God.

List below the first three personal aspirations and personal goals that come to your mind.

My personal aspirations and goals:

Pray, asking God to direct your passions toward Him.

Ask God to help you lay aside whatever agenda you may have for meeting the needs you listed above. Ask Him to guide you through the journey of making His will the main passion in your life and to help you trust in Him.

Executing the One-Day Fast

Begin your one-day, water-only fast immediately following today's evening meal (the last meal of the your day). You will continue your fast until it is broken with "break-fast" on Day Five of this week.

Documenting my Perspective During My Fasting

Use the space below to journal today's experiences as you begin your fast.

Journal

Record ideas, impressions, feelings, questions, and any insights you may have had during today's time.

Prayer

Pray for each member of your community.

Being Led by God Through Temptation to Transformation

DAY FOUR

Prayer

Dear Lord, I have a hard enough time resisting temptations which cross my path in a normal day's running that I don't need another source of temptation! For me, saying the "Devil made me do it" is just another excuse. Okay, I know that the Bible says the Devil is real. I get a little comfort by thinking that the Devil doesn't bother with small-potatoes Christians like me. So you can see that I get a little uncomfortable with the idea of attracting his attention. I'm fearful of what might happen once I begin to think and act like Jesus. Please protect me. Amen.

Core Thought

> For temptation to be transformational even the tempter must be an instrument of God's purposes.

C. S. Lewis begins the preface to his book *The Screwtape Letters* with the following observation:

> There are two equal and opposite errors into which our race can fall about the devils. One is to disbelieve in their existence. The other is to believe, and to feel an excessive and unhealthy interest in them. They themselves [the devils] are equally pleased by both errors and hail a materialist or a magician with the same delight.[1]

1. C. S. Lewis, *Screwtape Letters with Screwtape Proposes a Toast* (New York: Macmillian Company, 1961), 9.

We will not fall in to either error. That there indeed are devils, we do believe; that there is a devil, Satan, who delights in our downfall, the Scriptures clearly affirm: "Your enemy the devil prowls around like a roaring lion looking for someone to devour" (1 Peter 5:8). Our interest in demonic power is only for the sake of understanding the role the Devil may play in our temptation and the extent of his power.

From what is said in Scripture, we see that the Devil is powerful, knowledgeable, and apt at making his presence felt. Where he is mentioned, he most often is engaged in using his powers to tempt someone to sin (e.g., Adam and Eve, and Job). He is for this reason called "the tempter" (Matthew 4:3). Though powerful and knowledgeable, he is not all-powerful nor all-knowing nor able to know and act everywhere at any time; only God is and can do so.

A mistake made by many is to think of the Devil as the opposite of God or Jesus. But this is a serious mistake. The Devil is a creature and as such will never be the Father or the Son's equal. The important thing to remember is that the Devil's powers are limited and that his ability to exercise these limited powers is also limited. God has not given him permission to freely use it. The Devil does not have permission to do anything he desires to anyone he wishes, or tempt anyone at anytime he so schemes (Job 1:6-12). If the Devil is to tempt a believer, it will only be with God's permission, according to His rules, under His watchful eyes. Martin Luther reminds us that God works with all things such that they accomplish His will, even Satan, "lest you forget that the Devil is God's devil."[2]

Seeing the Devil in this light reveals that Satan at his worst is just another (though powerful) tool in God's hand, being used by the Father to accomplish what He does best, transforming believers into servants.

What may be taken away from all of this talk of devils, powers, and tools is this: the most important matter is not from *where* or from *whom* temptation comes or to *what* we are being tempted. What matters is that to live as Jesus lived, we must train ourselves to respond to *whatever*

---

2. Martin Luther, *Theologia Germanica* (Kila, MT: Kessinger Publishing, 2005), 42.

temptation, from *wherever*, with the same resistant resolve that Jesus showed. In our next meeting we discuss our need for voice-training.

Today's Exercises

Core Scripture: Matthew 4:1-2

Read aloud Matthew 4:1-2.

Recite this week's memory verse aloud five times.

> No temptation has seized you except what is common to man. And God is faithful; he will not let you be tempted beyond what you can bear. But when you are tempted, he will also provide a way out so that you can stand up under it. (1 Corinthians 10:13)

Meditate on today's passage.

Request to Be in His Presence

"Dear Lord, bring me into the context of Your world."

1. *Read it*—Remember: We read now only what is there, to hear once again, only what was spoken then.

    Read Matthew 4:1-2 (again) at least twice, out loud.

2. *Think it*—select a portion (you know what to do now), a phrase within the reading, and mull it over in your mind, thinking about the context and setting, reimagining the event, putting yourself into the situation. As you meditate, use all five senses to re-create the context and the setting by building the images that are supplied within the passages.

3. *Pray it*—ask God to give you understanding into how the truths He has spoken in these Scriptures apply to you now. Ask, "What is it about me that I need to deal with? What is it about me that must change?"

    Respond to God by accepting and admitting whatever responsibility is implied by what He has shown. Write what it is that God has shown you, and what you must admit responsibility for having done (or not done).

4. *Live it*—ask God to reveal to you what He wants you to do about what you have admitted.

List what particular action(s) you will take today to accomplish what God has revealed for you to do.

Pray, asking the Holy Spirit to empower you to act in obedience and to accomplish what He has revealed for you to do today.

Doing the Discipline: Continuing the One-Day Fast
Documenting My Perspective During My Fasting

Journal

Record ideas, impressions, feelings, questions, and any insights you may have had during today's time.

Prayer

Pray for each member of your community.

Being Led by God Through Temptation to Transformation

DAY FIVE

Prayer

Dear Lord, I want to be able to hear Your voice and have conversations with You throughout my day. I would love to hear what You have to say about the things that pop up as I conduct my routine. That is the kind of exciting, intimate relationship I have truly desired for a long time. Unfortunately, I'm as far from having that kind of relationship with You as I was when I first desired it. To be honest, I can't really tell if it's Your voice that is speaking to me, my own, or who knows what! Please help me to recognize your voice. Amen.

Core Thought

> To live as Jesus lived, we must train ourselves to recognize God's voice, and to follow only His leading.

The sheep listen to his voice. He calls his own sheep by name and leads them. . . . His sheep follow him because they know his voice. But they will never follow a stranger . . . because they do not recognize a stranger's voice. . . . I am the good shepherd. I know my sheep and my sheep know me. (John 10:1-14)

Today we will discuss what is imperative for temptation to be transformational, the ability to recognize God's voice, regardless of the circumstances. Within our electronically enabled consumer culture there are so many voices competing so loudly for our attention that our hearing is dulled by the roar of the crowd. And with so many different voices commanding us, it has become hard to tell who is saying what. Yet it is within this oppressive loudness that the Spirit of God speaks to us, expecting us to follow the leading of His "still small voice" (1 Kings 19:12, KJV). Unless we are able to hear and recognize His voice, we will not listen to His calling, trust His leading, or obey His directives, and we will not follow Him. So, the urgent questions that must be answered are: how we can hear the sound of God's voice beneath the roar, and how will we be able to recognize His voice when we do hear it and match His voice to His message? The answer to all these questions is that we must train to hear and recognize God's voice.

In the following weeks, you will learn and engage in specific practices that will aid you in training. We will introduce the practice of stilling to help you become able to hear God's voice. We will continue the discipline of meditating on God's Word using *lectio divina* to help you recognize the way God speaks. We will also study portions of Scripture to become familiar with the way God thinks.

To live as Jesus lived, we must train to hear and recognize the Father's voice by reserving times of quiet solitude to meditate on His Word, sit in stillness listening for Him, conversing with Him in prayer expecting His replies, and studying His Word becoming familiar with the way He thinks.

Today's Exercises

Core Scripture: Matthew 4:1-2
Read aloud Matthew 4:1-2.
Recite this week's memory verse aloud five times.

No temptation has seized you except what is common to man. And God is faithful; he will not let you be tempted beyond what you can bear. But when you are tempted, he will also provide a way out so that you can stand up under it. (1 Corinthians 10:13)

Meditate on today's passage.

Request to Be in His Presence
"Dear Lord, bring me into the context of Your world."

1. ***Read it***—Remember: We read now only what is there, to hear once again, only what was spoken then.

   Read Matthew 4:1-2 at least twice, out loud.

2. ***Think it***—select a portion, a phrase within the reading, and mull it over in your mind, thinking about the context and setting, reimagining the event, putting yourself into the situation. As you meditate, use all five senses to re-create the context and the setting by building the images that are supplied within the passages.

3. ***Pray it***—ask God to give you understanding into how the truths He has spoken in these Scriptures apply to you now. Ask, "What is it about me that I need to deal with? What is it about me that must change?"

   Respond to God by accepting and admitting whatever responsibility is implied by what He has shown. Write what it is that God has shown you, and what you must admit responsibility for having done (or not done).

4. ***Live it***—ask God to reveal to you what He wants you to do about what you have admitted.

   List what particular action(s) you will take today to accomplish what God has revealed for you to do.

Pray, asking the Holy Spirit to empower you to act in obedience and to accomplish what He has revealed for you to do today.

Doing the Discipline: Breaking the One-Day Fast

Deriving the Profit from My Fasting

Last week, we learned that for fasting to be transformational it must be practiced, that you have to do it, and, we just did. Also, we must review what we experienced during our fasting. We do this to clarify for ourselves what God intends that we understand from these experiences and what He expects us to do as the result of our understanding. Today we complete the fast by deriving from it the benefits that God intends for us to enjoy.

Start by reviewing the journal entries that you made:

1. Read each statement and ask yourself, "What did I mean when I wrote this down?"
2. Using the space below, answer the question, "What did I experience?"

"What do I know now from these experiences?"

3. Ask the Lord the following questions and write whatever comes to your mind as the result.

"Lord, what do you want me to learn from these experiences?"

"Lord, what do you want me to do with what I now know?"

Write a short summary of what you experienced while preparing, executing, and breaking your one-day fast.

Write a short statement of what you learned and what you believe God is leading you to do with what you have learned from your fast.

Journal

Record ideas, impressions, feelings, questions, and any insights you may have had during today's time.

Prayer

Pray for each member of your community.

Being Led by God Through Temptation to Transformation

DAY SIX

Community Meeting

In preparation for this week's meeting, you will have read and reflected upon each of the week's five Core Thoughts, recorded your thoughts and observations, and are ready to recite this week's memory verses to the group.

WEEK THREE

Being Led by Our Appetites: Catering to Cravings of Our Body

DAY ONE

Prayer

Dear Lord, I want to honor You with my all of me. I don't want my body to be used as a weapon against Your will being accomplished in my life. Please make me wise about how my body's feelings can be used in temptation by the Devil. Help me to stand against him and all his ways. Help me to use my body to bring honor to You. Amen.

Core Thought

> The Devil will devise temptations through his extraordinary creativity and determination to distort and interrupt our relationship with God and our understanding and accomplishing of our mission.

The Devil is a highly motivated, extraordinarily creative, and determined terrorist. He has identified the targets he must destroy and devises the weapons he will use to accomplish his terrorist mission: to distort and interrupt our relationship with God and distract us from our mission—doing God's will God's way.

A terrorist is one who uses violence, intimidation, coercion, and fear against civilians in order to attain goals that are political, ideological, or religious in nature. There is no greater terrorist than the Devil. Before he was defeated by Christ, the Devil's political goal was the rejection of God and His rule by all of creation. His ideological goal was establishing his rule over all creation. His religious goal was the recognition of himself as lord over all creation by all. Because of the ultimately devastating defeat he received at the hands of Jesus Christ, the risen Son of God, he now engages in terrorism to salvage what he can from the ruins of his aspirations. He has lost the war, so he has settled on avenging himself. He will find a way to make God pay. The Devil knows that he cannot attack God directly (even he knows the very notion is ridiculous), but he knows how to make God suffer. He will attack God's children—us. It helps that we know the Devil's goal and his ways. We see what he tried to do with God's Son, and we see how he tried to go about it. Knowing how Jesus responded to the Devil's attack is the key to launching our own offensive against him.

For the remainder of the week we will examine how the Devil seeks to destroy us by using our flesh (our body and its natural desires) to accomplish his will his way.

Today's Exercises
Core Scripture: Matthew 4:3-4
Read aloud Matthew 4:3-4.
Recite this week's memory verses aloud five times.

> Therefore do not let sin reign in your mortal body so that you obey its evil desires. Do not offer the parts of your body to sin, as instruments of wickedness, but rather offer yourselves to God, as those who have been brought from death to life; and offer the parts of your body to him as instruments of righteousness. For sin shall not be your master, because you are not under law, but under grace. (Romans 6:12-14)

Meditate on today's passage.

Request to Be in His Presence
"Dear Lord, bring me into the context of Your world."

1. ***Read it***—Remember: We read now only what is there, to hear once again, only what was spoken then.

    Read Matthew 4:3-4 at least twice, out loud.

2. ***Think it***—select a portion, a phrase within the reading, and mull it over in your mind, thinking about the context and setting, reimagining the event, putting yourself into the situation. As you meditate, use all five senses to re-create the context and the setting by building the images that are supplied within the passages.

3. ***Pray it***—ask God to give you understanding into how the truths He has spoken in these Scriptures apply to you now. Ask, "What is it about me that I need to deal with? What is it about me that must change?"

    Respond to God by accepting and admitting whatever responsibility is implied by what He has shown. Write what it is that God has shown you, and what you must admit responsibility for having done (or not done).

4. ***Live it***—ask God to reveal to you what He wants you to do about what you have admitted.

    List what particular action(s) you will take today to accomplish what God has revealed for you to do.

Pray, asking the Holy Spirit to empower you to act in obedience and to accomplish what He has revealed for you to do today.

Journal

Record ideas, impressions, feelings, questions, and any insights you may have had during today's time.

Prayer

Pray for each member of your community.

Being Led by Our Appetites: Catering to Cravings of Our Body

DAY TWO

Prayer

Dear Lord, it's easy for me to feel that all is well when my physical needs are being met. I often do whatever is required to satisfy its hungers. I've never considered whether always making sure my body gets what it wants might not be what You want me to do, that I might be missing something else that You know I really need. Please teach me what I need to know about and do regarding my body to make it something that I can use to worship you. Amen.

Core Thought

> When our body speaks to us, we need to listen . . .
> but not always. When our body commands us,
> we must subject it to our will and our will to Christ.

The Devil's principal method is deception, his principal tactic is distortion, and if all else fails he can still succeed by distraction. One of the Devil's most used and most successful means of distraction is to use our body's feelings to tempt us.

The Devil enjoys using our body's natural, God-given urges and responses as weapons to cause self-inflicted damage to our bodies and trauma to our souls. Where he can't accomplish our destruction, he can usually distract us from our mission. This is precisely what he was trying to do with Jesus when they met in the wilderness of temptation.

Scripture says that after forty days Jesus was hungry and the Devil makes what sounds like quite a reasonable suggestion: "Go on . . . You know how . . . what's the big deal? . . . we're not talking about something evil . . . when You're hungry it's the time to eat! God made You like that, didn't He? So, He expects it. Do it now!" The temptation is for Jesus to act now, to start acting like the Son of God now by changing stones into bread. The Devil was saying, "Because You are the most important Person on earth, then what You desire is also the most important thing on earth. So, if You're hungry, then the most important thing to be done now is to satisfy your hunger. You have the desire and the power to satisfy the desire, so use Your power and satisfy Your hunger—it's the most important thing right now. You can go back to your fast and discovering God's will, later."

Jesus knows that it was the Spirit of God who led Him into the wilderness and it would be the Spirit of God who would provide for Him there. By saying that "man does not live by bread alone," Jesus was not suggesting that man does not need bread at all. Rather, he was stating that God knows that we need food and drink to remain healthy, but that there is never a time when the growl of our stomach's voice should be obeyed before or without regard to all else that the Lord has said or may be trying to say to us. In short, what comes out of God's mouth is always more important than what goes into ours.

Today's Exercises

Core Scripture: Matthew 4:3-4
Read aloud Matthew 4:3-4.
Recite this week's memory verses aloud five times.

> Therefore do not let sin reign in your mortal body so that you obey its evil desires. Do not offer the parts of your body to sin, as instruments of wickedness, but rather offer yourselves to God, as those who have been brought from death to life; and offer the parts of your body to him as instruments of righteousness. For sin shall not be your master, because you are not under law, but under grace. (Romans 6:12-14)

Meditate on today's passage.

Request to Be in His Presence

"Dear Lord, bring me into the context of Your world."

1. ***Read it***—Remember: We read now only what is there, to hear once again, only what was spoken then.

   Read Matthew 4:3-4 at least twice, out loud.

2. ***Think it***—select a portion, a phrase within the reading, and mull it over in your mind, thinking about the context and setting, reimagining the event, putting yourself into the situation. As you meditate, use all five senses to re-create the context and the setting by building the images that are supplied within the passages.

3. ***Pray it***—ask God to give you understanding into how the truths He has spoken in these Scriptures apply to you now. Ask, "What is it about me that I need to deal with? What is it about me that must change?"

   Respond to God by accepting and admitting whatever responsibility is implied by what He has shown. Write what it is that God has shown you, and what you must admit responsibility for having done (or not done).

4. ***Live it***—ask God to reveal to you what He wants you to do about what you have admitted.

   List what particular action(s) you will take today to accomplish what God has revealed for you to do.

Pray, asking the Holy Spirit to empower you to act in obedience and to accomplish what He has revealed for you to do today.

Journal

Record ideas, impressions, feelings, questions, and any insights you may have had during today's time.

Prayer

Pray for each member of your community.

Being Led by Our Appetites:
Catering to Cravings of Our Body

DAY THREE

Prayer

Dear Father, I know that I like my food when I want it the way I want it. I like the taste of my favorite foods so much that I often eat too much of them. It is also true that when I'm hungry I can do little else until I eat. I sometimes look forward more to the big lunch I'm going to be having than the Sunday morning message that precedes it. Please help me live a life that shows that I truly value You and desire to live the way that pleases You. Amen.

Core Thought

> There are other sources of sustenance;
> we need not "live by bread alone."

Gluttony is the habit of being excessively devoted to consuming food and drink. The Hebrew word for gluttony, *zolel*, means to "to shake out," "to squander"; and hence describes one who wastes his own body (Deuteronomy 21:20). Our culture's excessive devotion to food is apparent.

Previously, our culture used food when we celebrated something. The enjoyment of food enhanced whatever we celebrated. We feasted because we shared in the celebration together; we had a festival. The sharing of food was used to heighten the enjoyment of something else, whatever we celebrated. Today, we celebrate food.

We have elevated the value of food from its use as a means for celebrating during a festival to the object we are valuing by devoting a festival to celebrate it.

That we are devoted to food can be seen by how we show our valuing of it: we learn to prepare and present it in exotic ways; we hope to
develop an informed appreciation for it; we become *connoisseurs*. We
dedicate special times of appreciation for it: wine-tasting parties, cheese
parties, and the barbecue. Food has become our religion.

If food has become our religion and gluttony (the practice of
worshipping food) is the sign of true devotion, then it should not be
surprising that we should begin to think of food the same way we used
to think about God.

We used to celebrate God who comforts, rewards, and heals us.
Now we celebrate food: we have comfort foods, prize foods, and we call
some healthy foods as if, like God, they have the power to give comfort,
acclaim, and to heal.

If it is an overstatement to say that we worship food, then at least
we should admit that we have devoted a great deal of our energy and
resources in using food to satisfy the unmet needs deep within us. Now
we are trying to satisfy ourselves through the right foods where before
we knew that only by being rightly related to the God who made us
would our deepest hunger be satisfied: "Blessed are those who hunger
and thirst for righteousness, for they will be filled" (Matthew 5:6).

Today's Exercises

Core Scripture: Matthew 4:3-4
Read aloud Matthew 4:3-4.
Recite this week's memory verses aloud five times.

> Therefore do not let sin reign in your mortal body so that you
> obey its evil desires. Do not offer the parts of your body to
> sin, as instruments of wickedness, but rather offer yourselves
> to God, as those who have been brought from death to life;
> and offer the parts of your body to him as instruments of righ-
> teousness. For sin shall not be your master, because you are not
> under law, but under grace. (Romans 6:12-14)

Meditate on today's passage.

Request to Be in His Presence

"Dear Lord, bring me into the context of Your world."

1. **Read it**—Remember: We read now only what is there, to hear once again, only what was spoken then.

   Read Matthew 4:3-4 at least twice, out loud.

2. **Think it**—select a portion, a phrase within the reading, and mull it over in your mind, thinking about the context and setting, reimagining the event, putting yourself into the situation. As you meditate, use all five senses to re-create the context and the setting by building the images that are supplied within the passages.

3. **Pray it**—ask God to give you understanding into how the truths He has spoken in these Scriptures apply to you now. Ask, "What is it about me that I need to deal with? What is it about me that must change?"

   Respond to God by accepting and admitting whatever responsibility is implied by what He has shown. Write what it is that God has shown you, and what you must admit responsibility for having done (or not done).

4. **Live it**—ask God to reveal to you what He wants you to do about what you have admitted.

   List what particular action(s) you will take today to accomplish what God has revealed for you to do.

Pray, asking the Holy Spirit to empower you to act in obedience and to accomplish what He has revealed for you to do today.

Journal

Record ideas, impressions, feelings, questions, and any insights you may have had during today's time.

Prayer

Pray for each member of your community.

Being Led by Our Appetites: Catering to Cravings of Our Body

DAY FOUR

Prayer

Dear Lord, I tend to live in the moment. By that I mean whatever happens to be drawing my attention at the moment is usually the thing I do something about. If I'm hungry, whatever else I may be doing is interrupted to deal with hunger. When my stomach growls, I take care of it. Help me to know when I should make eating a priority and when it should take a backseat to doing something else You may have for me to do. Amen.

Core Thought

> For Jesus, fasting is feasting on other food.

There are times when we know in general what we are to do. What we lack is the detail: what in particular should I do next, how should I go about it, and what are the steps that must be accomplished to reach the end? The same is often true regarding being led by the Spirit of God.

Usually when we feel the Spirit's leading, we get a general sense of what we are to do, but we lack the details. We see this also where Jesus is led by the Spirit into the wilderness.

From the text alone, we can see nothing other than Jesus obediently following the Spirit's leading into the wilderness, but we don't see any evidence that Jesus knew what lay ahead. A natural reading of the text leads us to believe that Jesus was unaware that He would be engaged in a face-to-face struggle of temptation with the Devil. What we do see is Jesus obeying God's leading, His going, and His being hungry from a long fast. The picture being painted for us shows how a faithful servant responds to the leading of the Holy Spirit. If we are to be faithful servants we will understand and respond likewise.

Jesus responded to the specific leading of the Spirit by going into the wilderness. But what was He to do now? He responded to this lack of detail by taking the opportunity that the solitude of the wilderness provided to ask God, "What is Your will for Me now?" What we fail to appreciate is the strong connection made between Jesus' being led into solitude to inquire about God's will and His being engaged in the practice of fasting. Jesus modeled abstaining from the company of others and abstaining from food for the purpose of seeking God's will.

This teaches abstention for a purpose. Jesus abstained from company to be exclusively attentive to only one Person, the Father. Jesus abstained from food to be wholly attentive to the desires of only one Person, His Father. For Jesus, knowing and doing the will of God is the most satisfying experience man can enjoy. "My food," said Jesus, "is to do the will of him who sent me and to finish his work" (John 4:34). Unlike "bread alone," this food will strengthen and bring satisfaction to body and soul forever.

Today's Exercises
Core Scripture: Matthew 4:3-4
Read aloud Matthew 4:3-4.
Recite this week's memory verses aloud five times.

> Therefore do not let sin reign in your mortal body so that you obey its evil desires. Do not offer the parts of your body to sin, as instruments of wickedness, but rather offer yourselves to God, as those who have been brought from death to life; and offer the parts of your body to him as instruments of righteousness. For sin shall not be your master, because you are not under law, but under grace. (Romans 6:12-14)

Meditate on today's passage.

Request to Be in His Presence
"Dear Lord, bring me into the context of Your world."

1. **Read it**—Remember: We read now only what is there, to hear once again, only what was spoken then.
   Read Matthew 4:3-4 at least twice, out loud.
2. **Think it**—select a portion, a phrase within the reading, and mull it over in your mind, thinking about the context and setting, reimagining the event, putting yourself into the situation. As you meditate, use all five senses to re-create the context and the setting by building the images that are supplied within the passages.
3. **Pray it**—ask God to give you understanding into how the truths He has spoken in these Scriptures apply to you now. Ask, "What is it about me that I need to deal with? What is it about me that must change?"
   Respond to God by accepting and admitting whatever responsibility is implied by what He has shown. Write what it is that God has shown you, and what you must admit responsibility for having done (or not done).
4. **Live it**—ask God to reveal to you what He wants you to do about what you have admitted.

List what particular action(s) you will take today to accomplish what God has revealed for you to do.

Pray, asking the Holy Spirit to empower you to act in obedience and to accomplish what He has revealed for you to do today.

Journal

Record ideas, impressions, feelings, questions, and any insights you may have had during today's time.

Prayer

Pray for each member of your community.

Being Led by Our Appetites: Catering to Cravings of Our Body

DAY FIVE

Prayer

Dear Lord, you know that I want what I want when I want it. And I usually want it right when I want it. Immediately. So when You want something else for me I hardly notice. I am easily satisfied by what I already like. Lord, open me up to experience the fullness of all that You can make of me. Give me the experiences that will change me into what You will. Let me taste and see that You are good. Amen.

Core Thought

> To live as Jesus lived, we must train our palate to prefer the satisfaction of other food.

We want to be satisfied and we want to enjoy becoming satisfied. The rub comes when in order to be satisfied we must do and experience things that we do not find enjoyable. What we really want is to have what we call our needs met by experiencing only what we find pleasurable. And it is right that we should want this: God has made us so.

God made us to enjoy Him and to have the pleasure of enjoying Him always. He intends that it should be so, and He has not changed His mind. And it would be so had something not changed. The something that changed was us.

Were it not for man's sin, we would be enjoying and pursuing the pleasure of God's presence. But the reality is we have changed. We no longer are as God made us, seeking the pleasure of His presence. We now desire the pleasure apart from His presence. To have it, we try to fill up on things that bring us pleasure in place of the One whose presence makes us whole. We will never be satisfied by filling ourselves with the things we find pleasurable. It is only by being filled with the presence of a person, our Maker, that we can be satisfied. We must be changed before we can enjoy the fullness of His presence. It is precisely this process that we must train ourselves to enjoy. By training we will develop a preference for doing what we do not now enjoy (God's will), for the sake of developing a preference for a Person (Jesus) whose presence we do not prefer.

The way we will learn to enjoy Jesus is by acquiring a taste for the things He enjoys. We must expand our palate to include the food He enjoys, which nourishes and sustains Him. His food is to do and accomplish the Father's will (John 4:34). But we must sometimes narrow our palate and abstain from one kind of food to fully know and appreciate Jesus' other food. Eating a particular kind of food is not evil, for "everything is permissible" says Paul, but "not everything is beneficial" (1 Corinthians 10:23). We are not to let food master us. By enjoying food and sometimes abstaining from it, we can develop a taste for Jesus' food. In this way you will "honor God with your body" (1 Corinthians 6:12-20).

Today's Exercises

Core Scripture: Matthew 4:3-4

Read aloud Matthew 4:3-4.

Recite this week's memory verses aloud five times.

> Therefore do not let sin reign in your mortal body so that you obey its evil desires. Do not offer the parts of your body to sin, as instruments of wickedness, but rather offer yourselves to God, as those who have been brought from death to life; and offer the parts of your body to him as instruments of righteousness. For sin shall not be your master, because you are not under law, but under grace. (Romans 6:12-14)

Meditate on today's passage.

Request to Be in His Presence

"Dear Lord, bring me into the context of Your world."

1. ***Read it***—Remember: We read now only what is there, to hear once again, only what was spoken then.

   Read Matthew 4:3–4 at least twice, out loud.

2. ***Think it***—select a portion, a phrase within the reading, and mull it over in your mind, thinking about the context and setting, reimagining the event, putting yourself into the situation. As you meditate, use all five senses to re-create the context and the setting by building the images that are supplied within the passages.

3. ***Pray it***—ask God to give you understanding into how the truths He has spoken in these Scriptures apply to you now. Ask, "What is it about me that I need to deal with? What is it about me that must change?"

   Respond to God by accepting and admitting whatever responsibility is implied by what He has shown. Write what it is that God has shown you, and what you must admit responsibility for having done (or not done).

4. ***Live it***—ask God to reveal to you what He wants you to do about what you have admitted.

List what particular action(s) you will take today to accomplish what God has revealed for you to do.

Pray, asking the Holy Spirit to empower you to act in obedience and to accomplish what He has revealed for you to do today.

Doing the Discipline: Preparing for the Three-Day Fast
Determining the Purpose of My Fast
This week we will begin to prepare for the second fast we will be engaging in the over the course of *Book Two.* This next fast will be a three-day, water-only fast that will begin the evening of Day Two of next week.

The first step in preparing for the three-day fast is for you to determine the purpose of your fasting (as was described in Week One). Use the following steps to help you determine the purpose of your fast.

1. Pray that God will direct you in determining the purpose, what issue you are seeking God's directing about.
2. Review the questions we provided to help you determine the spiritual area in your life you will be focusing on during the three-day fast.
3. Write a paragraph describing the issues you will be addressing in your fast, and the outcome you desire (in the space below).

The purpose of my fast, the issue on which I will focus and about which I will ask God's direction is:

Journal

Record ideas, impressions, feelings, questions, and any insights you may have had during today's time.

Prayer

Pray for each member of your community.

Being Led by Our Appetites:
Catering to the Cravings of Our Body

DAY SIX

Community Meeting

In preparation for this week's meeting, you will have read and reflected upon each of the week's five Core Thoughts, recorded your thoughts and observations, and are ready to recite this week's memory verses to the group.

WEEK FOUR

Being Led by Our Ego: Trusting in Our Skillfulness

DAY ONE

Prayer

Dear Lord, I'm not very good at trusting. I'm not comfortable with letting go and allowing others to do the best they can because often I can do it better. Often I take on more than I should because others have commented on how well it gets done when I do it. I have been disappointed and left to pick up the pieces when others have not kept their commitments. I have not become this way overnight. It is hard for me to trust in someone else's knowledge or commitment. And I suppose it's hard for me to trust You for the same reasons. I want to be able to relax and trust You. Help me. Amen.

Core Thought

> Our propensity to trust in our own talent and skill
> and to listen to other talented voices above depending
> upon God and before seeking His voice is idolatry.

The Devil tempting Jesus to "throw yourself down" was nothing other than an attempt to turn Him from serving His Father as His Lord to being served by His Father as His Lord. In effect, the Devil was saying to Jesus that because He was indeed the Son of God, He should expect (even as the Scriptures say) that everyone, including God the Father, would jump into action to serve His best interests. He should trust His own understanding of the Scriptures, His own position as the Son of God, and of course the advice of the most wise counselor, Satan. To do otherwise was to allow the Father to fail to serve the Son. And that would be unloving.

Jesus was not incapable of being persuaded to exercise His power and authority to make everyone jump when He jumped. Jesus was simply not willing to be persuaded. He chose to rely completely upon His Father to direct Him. He had trained Himself to be completely dependent upon God the Father to direct Him as to what He must do to accomplish the Father's will. He would wait to act until the Father told Him how He was to do His will. To do otherwise, to presume that one's own knowledge, position, and power are sufficient to truly know and rightly do God's will, was to Jesus' mind blasphemy. And to expect the Father to act in dutiful response to a man's will is to place the creature above the Creator, which is idolatry. Likewise to trust in sufficiency of our own or in any other person's understanding, talent, and skills instead of seeking out and relying on God to reveal and perform His ways through us is to elevate ourselves above God. It is blasphemy to think it, idolatry to do it, and damnable to believe it.

Today's Exercises
Core Scripture: Matthew 4:5-7
Read aloud Matthew 4:5-7.
Recite this week's memory verses aloud five times.

> Trust in the LORD with all your heart and lean not on your own understanding; in all your ways acknowledge him, and he will make your paths straight. Do not be wise in your own eyes; fear the LORD and shun evil. This will bring health to your body and nourishment to your bones. (Proverbs 3:5-8)

Meditate on today's passage.

Request to Be in His Presence
"Dear Lord, bring me into the context of Your world."

1. ***Read it***—Remember: We read now only what is there, to hear once again, only what was spoken then.

   Read Matthew 4:5-7 at least twice, out loud.

2. ***Think it***—select a portion, a phrase within the reading, and mull it over in your mind, thinking about the context and setting, reimagining the event, putting yourself into the situation. As you meditate, use all five senses to re-create the context and the setting by building the images that are supplied within the passages.

3. ***Pray it***—ask God to give you understanding into how the truths He has spoken in these Scriptures apply to you now. Ask, "What is it about me that I need to deal with? What is it about me that must change?"

   Respond to God by accepting and admitting whatever responsibility is implied by what He has shown. Write what it is that God has shown you, and what you must admit responsibility for having done (or not done).

4. ***Live it***—ask God to reveal to you what He wants you to do about what you have admitted.

   List what particular action(s) you will take today to accomplish what God has revealed for you to do.

Pray, asking the Holy Spirit to empower you to act in obedience and to accomplish what He has revealed for you to do today.

Doing the Discipline: Preparing for the Three-Day Fast
Determining the Privation of My Fast and Dedicating My Physical Self to God

The second step in preparing for the three-day fast has two parts. In part one, you will determine the *privation* of your fasting, what it is you will de-*prive* yourself of during your fast. Again, as you are learning the discipline of fasting, we have chosen the privation for this fast (i.e., privation of all foods). For now we will proceed to the second part, where you will dedicate your physical self, your body and its feelings and actions, as a living sacrifice to God.

Keeping your purpose in mind, write a prayer dedicating your body, its strength, health, and comfort, as a sacrifice to God. Acknowledge that He is the one who provides for your body, and state what it is that He provides for it. Tell Him why you are giving Him this time of fasting and that you give it freely whether your purpose is fulfilled or not, that what you desire more than the fulfilling of your purpose is to enjoy this time in His presence.

My Prayer of Dedication to You, Lord:

Journal

Record ideas, impressions, feelings, questions, and any insights you may have had during today's time.

Prayer

Pray for each member of your community.

Being Led by Our Ego: Trusting in Our Skillfulness

DAY TWO

Prayer

Dear Lord, sometimes when others compliment my work, I have a hard time just saying, "Thanks for noticing" without feeling like I'm being conceited. Other times, it will really bug me when I have done a really good job at something and no one seems to know that I did it. I know I shouldn't be like that. I can't help it. I like being the resident expert. Help me to know the right way to respond, how to be humble in the right way. Amen.

Core Thought

> There is great blessing and great danger in being greatly skilled.

Being highly skilled and using your skills to serve the Lord is a source of great blessing both to those who receive the benefits and to the one who gives of his skills. But there is also great danger to the greatly skilled and to the ones who are blessed.

There is great danger if one forgets that their great skills would never be were it not for God giving them other abilities, dispositions, and opportunities that allowed their development. For instance, one's skill in managing crisis situations may never have developed were it not for God giving the individual a naturally calm disposition. Or one's future skill as a neurosurgeon might never have developed were it not for God giving one extraordinary tactile dexterity and tremor-free hand-to-eye coordination. Ignoring this, the greatly skilled may begin to believe that their having greater skills which others greatly value means that they are of greater value than others and should be recognized and treated in ways that demonstrate their greater value. Here the greatly skilled person begins to believe a lie about himself, and begins to build his expectations as to how he ought to be treated by others upon this lie. We see that what God had intended to be used to serve and bring blessing to others was distorted. This skillfulness is being used by someone to gain an advantage over the ones for whom it was intended to serve. And rather than enjoying the thanks and praise of those who are blessed by his skillful service, the greatly skilled one becomes anxious in his concern to see that he is receiving the recognition appropriate to his value.

Forgetting that our skills are ultimately the result of God's gifting us for the purpose of expressing His love through our skillful service for others results in our positioning ourselves above those we are to serve. We are taking the place God alone is worthy to occupy.

In the same way, it is dangerous for those who receive the benefits at the hands of someone who is greatly skilled. The receiver may begin to value the benefit he receives from the skilled person more than he values the person with the skills. This is to value a person as only the means to one's own personal gain. To treat any person as if his value lay chiefly as a means to our own personal gain is precisely how the Devil hoped to use Jesus in this temptation. For us to do likewise is to dare to incite the anger of the Father, for He loves each of us so.

Today's Exercises
Core Scripture: Matthew 4:5-7
Read aloud Matthew 4:5-7.
Recite this week's memory verses aloud five times.

> Trust in the LORD with all your heart and lean not on your own understanding; in all your ways acknowledge him, and he will make your paths straight. Do not be wise in your own eyes; fear the LORD and shun evil. This will bring health to your body and nourishment to your bones. (Proverbs 3:5-8)

Meditate on today's passage.

Request to Be in His Presence

"Dear Lord, bring me into the context of Your world."

1. **Read it**—Remember: We read now only what is there, to hear
    once again, only what was spoken then.
    Read Matthew 4:5-7 at least twice, out loud.
2. **Think it**—select a portion, a phrase within the reading, and mull
    it over in your mind, thinking about the context and setting,
    reimagining the event, putting yourself into the situation. As you
    meditate, use all five senses to re-create the context and the setting
    by building the images that are supplied within the passages.
3. **Pray it**—ask God to give you understanding into how the truths
    He has spoken in these Scriptures apply to you now. Ask, "What
    is it about me that I need to deal with? What is it about me that
    must change?"
    Respond to God by accepting and admitting whatever
    responsibility is implied by what He has shown. Write what it is
    that God has shown you, and what you must admit responsibility
    for having done (or not done).
4. **Live it**—ask God to reveal to you what He wants you to do
    about what you have admitted.

List what particular action(s) you will take today to accomplish
what God has revealed for you to do.

Pray, asking the Holy Spirit to empower you to act in obedience and to
accomplish what He has revealed for you to do today.

Doing the Discipline: Preparing for the Three-Day Fast

Directing My Spirit's Passions Toward God

Today you will initiate the thee-day fast by beginning to direct your spirit's passion toward God.

List below the first three personal aspirations and personal goals that come to your mind.

My personal aspirations and goals:

Pray, asking God to direct your passions toward Him

Ask God to help you lay aside whatever agenda you may have for meeting the needs you listed above. Ask Him to guide you through the journey of making His will the main passion in your life and to help you trust in Him.

Executing the Three-Day Fast

Beginning this evening and continuing until the morning of Day Six, you will abstain from eating your last two meals of the day. You may eat your normal morning meal, but you are to skip the last two meals of the day. During the entirety of the fast you may drink water at any time. You will break your fast with "break-fast" the morning of Day Six of this week.

Journal

Record ideas, impressions, feelings, questions, and any insights you may have had during today's time.

Documenting My Perspective During My Fasting

Use the space below to journal today's experiences as you begin your fast.

Prayer

Pray for each member of your community.

Being Led by Our Ego:
Trusting in Our Skillfulness

DAY THREE

Prayer

Dear Father, I tend to trust my own thinking on just about everything. I sometimes won't ask for help, especially if I think it will diminish my standing in someone else's eyes. It seems to me that I want to serve You and rely on You to make me all I can be so long as I don't look like anything other than successful. Lord, I do want to be used by You, but I fear letting You or anyone else put me at risk. Please help me to trust Your understanding, direction, and love for me. Amen.

Core Thought

> Trusting in our talent and skill
> leads to great pride and a great fall.

I'm sure that the person most surprised that Jesus did not fall to the Devil's tempting was the Devil himself. I'm also confident that he rarely undergoes this kind of defeat. I speak from experience. Usually, all the Devil has to do to enable my failing when tempted is to present me with some reasonable justification to allow me to think that whatever is required by God's holiness does not apply to me in exactly the same way it does to others. By others, of course, I mean people who are neither as talented nor skilled or bright as I believe myself to be. The usual requirements for righteousness common for all Christians to perform do not apply to the special class of Christians to which I am a member. Why is the Devil usually successful? Because we like to believe the lies he tells us about ourselves.

I am easy prey for the Devil. What makes me so is that when the Devil tempts me with lies about my being more valuable than others and I start to feel good about it, I forget the most important fact about the Devil. I fail to keep in the forefront of my mind the one thing that motivates his having any interest in me at all.

The Devil is only interested in me as a means by which he can cause God to suffer. The Devil tells me lies to make me believe that I am superior to others, not because it makes me feel good about myself. He pumps up those prideful feelings because when I'm feeling good about being superior I am most willing to cause harm to others. I am seduced, of course, into believing that if others have been hurt by my superior attitude and actions it is actually a good thing. After all, the truth sometimes hurts.

Because the Devil can't cause God to suffer directly, he goes after us, knowing that our sinfulness can be incited through temptation to cause others (and ourselves) to suffer directly and God to suffer (indirectly) because of His love for us.

When God's children hurt others because of their inflamed pride, He finds it so grievous and destructive that He has committed Himself to act to suppress it: "Pride goes before destruction, a haughty spirit before a fall. Better to be lowly in spirit and among the oppressed than to share plunder with the proud" (Proverbs 16:18-19).

Today's Exercises
Core Scripture: Matthew 4:5-7
Read aloud Matthew 4:5-7.
Recite this week's memory verses aloud five times.

Trust in the LORD with all your heart and lean not on your own understanding; in all your ways acknowledge him, and he will make your paths straight. Do not be wise in your own eyes; fear the LORD and shun evil. This will bring health to your body and nourishment to your bones. (Proverbs 3:5-8)

Meditate on today's passage.

Request to Be in His Presence

"Dear Lord, bring me into the context of Your world."

1. ***Read it***—Remember: We read now only what is there, to hear once again, only what was spoken then.

    Read Matthew 4:5-7 at least twice, out loud.

2. ***Think it***—select a portion, a phrase within the reading, and mull it over in your mind, thinking about the context and setting, reimagining the event, putting yourself into the situation. As you meditate, use all five senses to re-create the context and the setting by building the images that are supplied within the passages.

3. ***Pray it***—ask God to give you understanding into how the truths He has spoken in these Scriptures apply to you now. Ask, "What is it about me that I need to deal with? What is it about me that must change?"

    Respond to God by accepting and admitting whatever responsibility is implied by what He has shown. Write what it is that God has shown you, and what you must admit responsibility for having done (or not done).

4. ***Live it***—ask God to reveal to you what He wants you to do about what you have admitted.

List what particular action(s) you will take today to accomplish what God has revealed for you to do.

Pray, asking the Holy Spirit to empower you to act in obedience and to accomplish what He has revealed for you to do today.

Doing the Discipline: Continuing the Three-Day Fast
Documenting My Perspective During My Fasting

Journal

Record ideas, impressions, feelings, questions, and any insights you may have had during today's time.

Prayer

Pray for each member of your community.

Being Led by Our Ego:
Trusting in Our Skillfulness

DAY FOUR

Prayer

Dear Lord, I've always associated weakness with following and strength with leading. In fact, what makes me most anxious is watching someone else perform poorly. I want to pick up whatever it was that they were trying to do and do it myself. I have the hardest time not feeling responsible for things to turn out right even when I'm not the one involved. My sign for having done something good has been that I got the expected outcome. When things don't work as expected I feel terrible even though I've done my best. Help me to be satisfied with doing Your will and letting the end product be Your responsibility. Amen.

Core Thought

> Trusting in our talent and skill leads
> to weak faith and an anxious life.

There is nothing dangerous about talent and skill. What is dangerous is our habit of becoming dependent upon the things that give us what we feel we need. Trusting in our talent and skill, as good as they may have served us in the past, sets us up for disappointment in the future.

If you are going to trust in talent and skill to make your future secure, you had better be about the business of always keeping your talent and skills in top form. But as we all know, there comes a time (that's right . . . in the future) when you simply cannot perform as well as in days gone by. You have trusted in the very thing that you know will not make your future secure. You have knowingly set yourself up for a life of hard work, keeping your skill level up, and anxiety, knowing that the time will come when your talent and skill will not be up to the task.

A faith that inhabits a life built upon the foundation of our talent and skill is as secure as a sandcastle at low tide. It may give us what we want now, but we know that it will show its true strength when the tide rises. And rise it will. The only truly secure and anxiety-free life is that which has faith firmly rooted in trusting Jesus, "He [who] commands even the winds and the water, and they obey Him" (Luke 8:25, NASB).

Today's Exercises

Core Scripture: Matthew 4:5-7

Read aloud Matthew 4:5-7.

Recite this week's memory verses aloud five times.

> Trust in the LORD with all your heart and lean not on your own understanding; in all your ways acknowledge him, and he will make your paths straight. Do not be wise in your own eyes; fear the LORD and shun evil. This will bring health to your body and nourishment to your bones. (Proverbs 3:5-8)

Meditate on today's passage.

Request to Be in His Presence

"Dear Lord, bring me into the context of Your world."

1. *Read it*—Remember: We read now only what is there, to hear once again, only what was spoken then.

   Read Matthew 4:5-7 at least twice, out loud.

2. *Think it*—select a portion, a phrase within the reading, and mull it over in your mind, thinking about the context and setting, reimagining the event, putting yourself into the situation. As you meditate, use all five senses to re-create the context and the setting

by building the images that are supplied within the passages.

3. *Pray it*—ask God to give you understanding into how the truths He has spoken in these Scriptures apply to you now. Ask, "What is it about me that I need to deal with? What is it about me that must change?"

Respond to God by accepting and admitting whatever responsibility is implied by what He has shown. Write what it is that God has shown you, and what you must admit responsibility for having done (or not done).

4. *Live it*—ask God to reveal to you what He wants you to do about what you have admitted.

List what particular action(s) you will take today to accomplish what God has revealed for you to do.

Pray, asking the Holy Spirit to empower you to act in obedience and to accomplish what He has revealed for you to do today.

Doing the Discipline: Continuing the Three-Day Fast
Documenting My Perspective During My Fasting

Journal

Record ideas, impressions, feelings, questions, and any insights you may have had during today's time.

Prayer

Pray for each member of your community.

Being Led by Our Ego: Trusting in Our Skillfulness

DAY FIVE

Prayer

Dear Lord, I want to grow into the kind of disciple that keeps doing whatever it is that You want done. I don't want to rely on the approval of others or even upon my own assessment as to my success. I desire to be motivated by pleasing only You. I know that this is going to be a life-long process of change for me, but in my heart of hearts this is what I desire. Bless me with the will and the power to do Your will Your way. Amen.

Core Thought

> To live as Jesus lived we must train ourselves not to trust in talent and skillfulness to accomplish the will of God but to become fully dependent upon God to accomplish His will through us and this even when it does not display our competency.

We came by it "honestly," that predisposition to trust in our own skillfulness rather than being fully dependent upon God to accomplish His will through us. It was the natural result of man's first fall to the Devil's tempting. It is the repeated sin of mankind ever since.

When Adam fell, the immediate result was his alienation from God. He hid. Subsequently, man has preferred to maintain his distance from God. We don't like reminders that we don't measure up. As a result, we have spent millennia trying to hone our skills to make it on our own, something which God never intended for us to do. We Christians continue this sin.

Christians, who ought to know better, continue to find some sort of romantic attraction to the notion of being "self-sufficient," of going it on your own, of being the self-reliant soul. This notion, as attractive as it may seem, is so contrary to the duty we have as Christians, to do God's will His way in His power in His time, that in pursuing it a Christian commits idolatry. The self-reliant Christian has set himself in God's place to be praised for his strength.

To live as Jesus lived we must reject what has come to us "honestly." We must live counter to our culture, which prizes a lone-wolf, rugged self-sufficient individualism. And we must train ourselves to live out our faith trusting in none other than God for our sustenance, security, and affirmation.

We've known all along that we could never *really* make it on own. We are God's creatures, "the work of His hand." God made us to experience joy when He is doing His work through us, as gleefully as the little child writing her name, with her tiny hand clasped within her father's directing hand. "For we are God's workmanship, created in Christ Jesus to do good works, which God prepared in advance for us to do" (Ephesians 2:10).

Today's Exercises

Core Scripture: Matthew 4:5-7

Read aloud Matthew 4:5-7.

Recite this week's memory verses aloud five times.

> Trust in the LORD with all your heart and lean not on your own understanding; in all your ways acknowledge him, and he will make your paths straight. Do not be wise in your own eyes; fear the LORD and shun evil. This will bring health to your body and nourishment to your bones. (Proverbs 3:5-8)

Meditate on today's passage.

Request to Be in His Presence

"Dear Lord, bring me into the context of Your world."

1. ***Read it***—Remember: We read now only what is there, to hear once again, only what was spoken then.

    Read Matthew 4:5-7 at least twice, out loud.

2. ***Think it***—select a portion, a phrase within the reading, and mull it over in your mind, thinking about the context and setting, reimagining the event, putting yourself into the situation. As you meditate, use all five senses to re-create the context and the setting by building the images that are supplied within the passages.

3. ***Pray it***—ask God to give you understanding into how the truths He has spoken in these Scriptures apply to you now. Ask, "What is it about me that I need to deal with? What is it about me that must change?"

    Respond to God by accepting and admitting whatever responsibility is implied by what He has shown. Write what it is that God has shown you, and what you must admit responsibility for having done (or not done).

4. ***Live it***—ask God to reveal to you what He wants you to do about what you have admitted.

List what particular action(s) you will take today to accomplish what God has revealed for you to do.

Pray, asking the Holy Spirit to empower you to act in obedience and to accomplish what He has revealed for you to do today.

Journal

Record ideas, impressions, feelings, questions, and any insights you may have had during today's time.

Doing the Discipline: Continuing the Three-Day Fast

Documenting My Perspective During My Fasting

Prayer

Pray for each member of your community.

Being Led by Our Ego:
Trusting in Our Skillfulness

DAY SIX

Community Meeting

In preparation for this week's meeting, you will have read and reflected upon each of the week's five Core Thoughts, recorded your thoughts and observations, and are ready to recite this week's memory verses to the group.

Doing the Discipline: Breaking the Three-Day Fast
Deriving the Profit from My Fasting

Start by reviewing the journal entries that you made:

1. Read each statement and ask yourself, "What did I mean when I wrote this down?"
2. Using the space below, answer the question "What did I experience?"

"What do I know now from these experiences?"

3. Ask the Lord the following questions and write whatever comes to your mind as the result.

"Lord, what do you want me to learn from these experiences?"

"Lord, what do you want me to do with what I now know?"

4. Write a short summary of what you experienced while preparing, executing, and breaking your three-day fast.

5. Write a short statement of what you learned and what you believe God is leading you to do with what you have learned from your fast.

WEEK FIVE

Being Led by the Crowd: Bowing to the Pressure of Impatience and Ambition

DAY ONE

Prayer

Dear Lord, I admit it, I look for shortcuts where I can find them. And though I'm not always pleased with the results, I still check to see if there is a shortcut before I waste my time having to do all the work. This is especially true about how I decide what to do regarding my spiritual growth. I just don't like having to commit to a long, drawn-out process. I wish there was a spiritual pill I could take that would do the trick. I know how immature that sounds, Lord, but that is what I feel. I want to do Your will Your way, but it's hard. Please help me to know what's wrong with me, and help me to do what You know is right for me. Amen.

Core Thought

> The lie of our manic culture is that the appearance of excellence is better than the reality, especially when it costs me little and gains me a lot.

The temptation offered by the Devil and rejected by Jesus was to the Devil a win-win proposition. Jesus would get what He wanted and of course the Devil would get his due . . . win-win. There seems to be many advantages to his proposal. The Devil says, "First, this whole thing could be wrapped up right here, right now, no long dragged-out ordeal . . . do it and we're done . . . win-win. Second, no more having to deal with the Jews or Romans or anyone else that gets in Your way, for that matter. You'll be calling all the shots. Third, no need for further embarrassments: who's to see? It's just You and me out here all alone. After that, no more being humiliated; You can speak your mind when and wherever You desire, no more fasting, sleepless nights, preaching campaigns, having to drag around twelve guys as dense as lead, and what's best, no Cross. Everything will be taken care of. It's a win-win situation. Just a little bow . . . say the words . . . nothing special . . . You know . . . something like, 'Lucifer is the king of kings and lord of lords. May He reign forever and ever.'" Win-win. What was offered was no pain, all gain. Tempting, yes, but successful? No.

As I imagine the encounter, I see the Devil's usual style of tempta-tion. He offers a quick-fix, one that appears to meet the need and at first glance, costs one very little. There was almost no pause between the Devil's words and Jesus' response. There was no time taken by Jesus to consider the advantages and ponder the opportunity. Jesus naturally responded out of the character that the practice of spiritual disciplines had produced within Him. He saw the splendor and heard the offer, but when the Devil stated the conditions "if you will bow down and worship me," for Jesus there was nothing real to consider. The word *worship* had meaning only with reference to God, His Father. Jesus trained, practiced, and understood it so.

When temptation called upon Jesus to choose, He responded not out of some momentary desire or to the pressure of the circumstances but from the solid character God had forged within Him.

Today's Exercises
Core Scripture: Matthew 4:8-9
Read aloud Matthew 4:8-9.
Recite this week's memory verses aloud five times.

Therefore, as God's chosen people, holy and dearly loved, clothe yourselves with compassion, kindness, humility, gentleness and patience. (Colossians 3:12)

Meditate on today's passage.

Request to Be in His Presence

"Dear Lord, bring me into the context of Your world."

1. **Read it**—Remember: We read now only what is there, to hear once again, only what was spoken then.

   Read Matthew 4:8-9 at least twice, out loud.

2. **Think it**—select a portion, a phrase within the reading, and mull it over in your mind, thinking about the context and setting, reimagining the event, putting yourself into the situation. As you meditate, use all five senses to re-create the context and the setting by building the images that are supplied within the passages.

3. **Pray it**—ask God to give you understanding into how the truths He has spoken in these Scriptures apply to you now. Ask, "What is it about me that I need to deal with? What is it about me that must change?"

   Respond to God by accepting and admitting whatever responsibility is implied by what He has shown. Write what it is that God has shown you, and what you must admit responsibility for having done (or not done).

4. **Live it**—ask God to reveal to you what He wants you to do about what you have admitted.

   List what particular action(s) you will take today to accomplish what God has revealed for you to do.

Pray, asking the Holy Spirit to empower you to act in obedience and to accomplish what He has revealed for you to do today.

Journal

Record ideas, impressions, feelings, questions, and any insights you may have had during today's time.

Prayer

Pray for each member of your community.

Being Led by the Crowd: Bowing to the Pressure of Impatience and Ambition

DAY TWO

Prayer

Dear Lord, I want to experience that abundant life You have for me to live. While I have had many wonderful experiences that I know came from You, I'm still waiting for the easy yoke and the rest You talked about. Help me know what to do and do what it takes to be obedient and faithful to You. Help me to stay with it until I get it. Amen.

Core Thought

> The work of spiritual formation is a slow work, so it can't be hurried. It is an urgent work, so it can't be delayed.

To live as Jesus lived means to respond to the issues and circumstances of life in ways that accomplish the will of God in the manner that pleases Him, doing His will His way. The object of spiritual formation is to replace the defective character which was formed by a sin-sick mind through sinful behaviors with a transformed character (one like Jesus'), the product of a renewed mind and spiritually disciplined behaviors. The task of forming within us the same kind of spiritual character that Jesus displayed cannot be accomplished through any quick-fix method. Any method that offers such should be rejected out of hand. Consideration of it is simply another waste of time. And time is exactly what we do not have to waste.

It is imperative for each Christian to be committed to and engaged in the process of spiritual formation. It is urgent that we begin the process immediately. It must not be delayed. To delay puts a Christian in a terrible position. As Christians, we are required to do God's will God's way, to live as Jesus lived: to be holy, righteous, and just in our dealings and to exhibit the fruit of the Spirit. But it is impossible for us to do God's will God's way, if all we have to direct our thoughts and behaviors is our defective character. Delaying also means that the principle way for us to be blessed, to enjoy our new life in Christ, is not yet available to us.

God designed and made us in such a way that fully enjoying the abundant life He has in store for each of us requires that we develop the desire and acquire a taste for doing God's will His way. We can only be truly satisfied by both desiring and doing what pleases God. To begin to enjoy our new, eternal life, we must begin to enjoy doing God's will, and to begin to enjoy doing God's will, we must begin by experiencing God's blessing. We experience God's blessing when we obey His commandments. The catch is that our current character does not help us to obey God's commands. In fact, it is the greatest obstacle to obedience to God. Therefore, because the entire process of forming Christ's character in us is a slow work that can't be hurried along by quick fixes, it is crucial that we do not delay its beginning. God wants us to enjoy our new life in Christ. He wants to bless us and for us to enjoy Him. To do so is to live as Jesus lived from His character formed in us.

Today's Exercises
Core Scripture: Matthew 4:8-9
Read aloud Matthew 4:8-9.
Recite this week's memory verses aloud five times.

> Therefore, as God's chosen people, holy and dearly loved, clothe yourselves with compassion, kindness, humility, gentleness and patience. (Colossians 3:12)

Meditate on today's passage.

Request to Be in His Presence

"Dear Lord, bring me into the context of Your world."

1. **Read it**—Remember: We read now only what is there, to hear once again, only what was spoken then.

   Read Matthew 4:8-9 at least twice, out loud.

2. **Think it**—select a portion, a phrase within the reading, and mull it over in your mind, thinking about the context and setting, reimagining the event, putting yourself into the situation. As you meditate, use all five senses to re-create the context and the setting by building the images that are supplied within the passages.

3. **Pray it**—ask God to give you understanding into how the truths He has spoken in these Scriptures apply to you now. Ask, "What is it about me that I need to deal with? What is it about me that must change?"

   Respond to God by accepting and admitting whatever responsibility is implied by what He has shown. Write what it is that God has shown you, and what you must admit responsibility for having done (or not done).

4. **Live it**—ask God to reveal to you what He wants you to do about what you have admitted.

   List what particular action(s) you will take today to accomplish what God has revealed for you to do.

Pray, asking the Holy Spirit to empower you to act in obedience and to accomplish what He has revealed for you to do today.

Journal

Record ideas, impressions, feelings, questions, and any insights you may have had during today's time.

Prayer

Pray for each member of your community.

Being Led by the Crowd: Bowing to the Pressure of Impatience and Ambition

DAY THREE

Prayer

Dear Father, I know I am impatient. I get impatient with family members who don't do what they say they will do. I also get impatient with people at work who tell me that they know they need to do something (usually something I need for them to get done) but they don't know if they will be able to get it done. Ughhhh! Why won't they just be honest with me and tell me that they don't want to do it, so they aren't going to do it. Instead, they string me along, and then I'm left to do it myself anyway. Say, Lord, do I do that to you? Okay, that's got to change. Lord, thank You for being patient with me. Amen.

Core Thought

> Godly character cannot be developed when ambition, fueled by impatience, moves us to seek affirmation by behaving in ways that are self-promoting.

One attitude that must be present for a Christian to develop godly character is a willingness to change. This willingness to change on the part of a Christian comes from his God-given conviction that what he is now is not what God wants him to be and a God-given desire to become all that God wants him to be. This God-given conviction and the desire to submit to God's will over one's own marks the beginning of godly character formation. It marks the presence of true humility, with small and faltering steps no doubt, but true humility nonetheless. Conviction and desire born out of humility are the motivators that allow the spiritual formation of godly character. The lacking of them guarantees its absence, and the supplanting of them with ambition and impatience imperils its growth.

Godly character cannot be developed in a person who is driven by ambition and in whom impatience rules. An ambitious person is one who uses other people to advance their position and personal agenda. An impatient person is one who believes that others are not properly recognizing and conforming their behaviors to adequately honor their value. The impatient person expresses his dissatisfaction with others in ways that show he believes himself to be of superior value. The reason why godly character cannot develop in ambitious or impatient persons is that each places themselves before all others. Neither the ambitious nor the impatient persons really believe that others are of equal value with them. They believe themselves to be superior.

The ambitious person seeks to be superior to others. He shows this by behaving in ways that indicate he believes that it is permissible for him to step on people if that will advance him to the position he desires and deserves above everyone else. The ambitious person uses people as things to suit his purposes.

The impatient person already believes himself to be superior. He shows this by behaving in ways that indicate only his own value and values must be respected. He is easily offended and reacts disrespectfully to those whom he believes have not accorded him the respect he feels is his due. It is hard to imagine attitudes more contrary to that which is seen in true humility. Humility requests, "Lord, may Your will be done." Ambition and impatience say, "Lord! My will be done."

Today's Exercises

Core Scripture: Matthew 4:8-9

Read aloud Matthew 4:8-9.

Recite this week's memory verses aloud five times.

Therefore, as God's chosen people, holy and dearly loved, clothe yourselves with compassion, kindness, humility, gentleness and patience. (Colossians 3:12)

Meditate on today's passage.

Request to Be in His Presence

"Dear Lord, bring me into the context of Your world."

1. ***Read it***—Remember: We read now only what is there, to hear once again, only what was spoken then.
   Read Matthew 4:8-9 at least twice, out loud.
2. ***Think it***—select a portion, a phrase within the reading, mull it over in your mind, thinking about the context and setting, reimagining the event, putting yourself into the situation. As you meditate, use all five senses to re-create the context and the setting by building the images that are supplied within the passages.
3. ***Pray it***—ask God to give you understanding into how the truths He has spoken in these Scriptures apply to you now. Ask, "What is it about me that I need to deal with? What is it about me that must change?"
   Respond to God by accepting and admitting whatever responsibility is implied by what He has shown. Write what it is that God has shown you, and what you must admit responsibility for having done (or not done).
4. ***Live it***—ask God to reveal to you what He wants you to do about what you have admitted.

List what particular action(s) you will take today to accomplish what God has revealed for you to do.

Pray, asking the Holy Spirit to empower you to act in obedience and to accomplish what He has revealed for you to do today.

Doing the Discipline: Preparing for the Five-Day Fast
Determining the Purpose of My Fast
Today we begin to prepare for the last fast we will be engaging in during *Book Two*. This is a five-day, water-only fast that will begin on the morning of Day One of Week Six. The fast will involve skipping the first two meals of each day and drinking only water for the duration of the fast.

Today you will establish the purpose for the five-day fast. Use the following steps to help you determine the purpose of your fast.

1. Pray that God will direct you in determining the purpose, what issue you are seeking God's direction about.
2. Review the questions we provided to help you determine the spiritual area in your life you will be focusing on during the five-day fast.
3. Write a paragraph describing the issues you will be addressing in your fast and the outcome you desire (in the space below).

The purpose of my fast, the issue upon which I will focus and about which I will ask God's direction is:

Journal

Record ideas, impressions, feelings, questions, and any insights you may have had during today's time.

Prayer

Pray for each member of your community.

Being Led by the Crowd: Bowing to the Pressure of Impatience and Ambition

DAY FOUR

Prayer

Dear Lord, I want to make good decisions. By that I mean make decisions based upon the truth. I know that my judgment as to what is true or good is oftentimes clouded by my desire to satisfy myself, to get what I want the way I want it. Many times when I did get what I so desperately wanted, it didn't satisfy me, so I wanted something newer or bigger, faster or flashier. But I keep experiencing the same disappointment. It's great when it's new, but then I don't want it anymore. It didn't satisfy. Lord, I'm starting to realize that there is something wrong with trying to be satisfied in this way. Help me, Lord, to find satisfaction Your way. Amen.

Core Thought

> Living the fast-food, "super-size me" life leads to spiritual death.

Our culture advances a creed that affirms the bigger and the faster, the better. We have been saturated by advertising that promotes this credo, and it has shaped our thinking in almost every area of our lives. It has also shaped our thinking in the area of spiritual growth.

When we shop for ways to develop our spiritual lives, more often than not we use the same criteria to determine which we will use as we do for choosing a car to purchase, diet to attempt, or shampoo to use.

The criteria we use reflects what we value.

Some questions that typically reflect the values of our consumer culture are: What will it give me? Will it do what I want it to do? How fast will it do it? How much do I like it? And will it give me the most bang for my buck? And to satisfy values implied by these criteria the answer must be, "It gives me what I want, and I want a lot, and I want it now!"

While these questions may be appropriate to ask about a product that we will own and use, they are wholly inappropriate for determining the proper method for *producing* someone else's product according to their design. The criteria are wrong, and the person making the determination is the wrong person.

It is as ridiculous to expect a sinner to be able to determine the best way to change himself from what he is into what God wants him to be as it is to depend upon a drug addict to recommend the best treatment to use to help him with his problem. We should not be surprised when he recommends that he be supplied with his drug of choice for as long as he wants it, that his problem, as far as he is concerned, is maintaining a ready supply of his drug, and that we can help by making sure he gets it. While he does recommend a solution that will give him what he wants, that will work for him, that he will like, and that gives him the most bang for his buck, his solution is not a remedy at all, and it will only magnify his real problem. His real problem is that his addiction has impaired his ability to choose what is in his own best interest. He cannot and should not be relied upon to choose the best course of treatment to break him of his addiction. Like the addict, we have so greatly consumed the values of our culture that it has impaired our ability to choose for ourselves the best means for forming Christ in us.

We risk destroying ourselves if we do not reject our culture's values and submit ourselves to God, our Owner and Designer, and become the product He intends to use to accomplish His will His way.

Today's Exercises

Core Scripture: Matthew 4:8-9

Read aloud Matthew 4:8-9.

Recite this week's memory verses aloud five times.

> Therefore, as God's chosen people, holy and dearly loved, clothe
> yourselves with compassion, kindness, humility, gentleness and
> patience. (Colossians 3:12)

Meditate on today's passage.

Request to Be in His Presence

"Dear Lord, bring me into the context of Your world."

1. **Read it**—Remember: We read now only what is there, to hear
   once again, only what was spoken then.
   Read Matthew 4:8-9 at least twice, out loud.
2. **Think it**—select a portion, a phrase within the reading, and mull
   it over in your mind, thinking about the context and setting,
   reimagining the event, putting yourself into the situation. As you
   meditate, use all five senses to re-create the context and the setting
   by building the images that are supplied within the passages.
3. **Pray it**—ask God to give you understanding into how the truths
   He has spoken in these Scriptures apply to you now. Ask, "What
   is it about me that I need to deal with? What is it about me that
   must change?"
   Respond to God by accepting and admitting whatever
   responsibility is implied by what He has shown. Write what it is
   that God has shown you, and what you must admit responsibility
   for having done (or not done).
4. **Live it**—ask God to reveal to you what He wants you to do
   about what you have admitted.

List what particular action(s) you will take today to accomplish what God has revealed for you to do.

Pray, asking the Holy Spirit to empower you to act in obedience and to accomplish what He has revealed for you to do today.

Doing the Discipline: Preparing for the Five-Day Fast
Dedicating My Physical Self to God
Today you will dedicate your physical self, your body and its feelings and actions, as a living sacrifice to God in preparation for your time of fasting.

Keeping your purpose in mind, write a prayer dedicating your body, its strength, health, and comfort, as a sacrifice to God. Acknowledge that He is the one who provides for your body, and state what it is that He provides for it. Tell Him why you are giving Him this time of fasting and that you give it freely whether your purpose is fulfilled or not, that what you desire more than the fulfilling of your purpose is to enjoy this time in His presence.

My Prayer of Dedication to You, Lord:

Journal

Record ideas, impressions, feelings, questions, and any insights you may have had during today's time.

Prayer

Pray for each member of your community.

Being Led by the Crowd:
Bowing to the Pressure of
Impatience and Ambition

DAY FIVE

Prayer

Dear Lord, I've learned much about myself and my ways this week. Please help me to do the things that I must do to become a disciple that truly enjoys doing Your will Your Way. Amen.

Core Thought

> We want it big, fast, and now. The Devil has been unsuccessful in his previous attempts to tempt Jesus. He now tries one of his most successful methods of temptation. He field-tested it with Adam and Eve, and it proved so successful that he's used it widely ever since.

The Devil tempts us by playing upon a sentiment all Christians maintain. Christians say they want to do the will of God. We say it because we know God's will is what we ought to be doing whether we want to or not. But because we most often do not, we make a little door of respectability that allows us to sneak out of the lie we are telling, "I said I *wanted* to do God's will, but sometimes I just can't make myself do it . . . it's too hard for me." Let's not kid ourselves. The last statement boils down to, "I know what I ought to do, but most of the time I decide I won't do it." It doesn't project as nice a sentiment when you juxtapose "ought to" and "won't do," but it is the truth. We know we ought to do God's will, but we know we do not want to do it, so we know that we will decide not to do it. It is at this point that the Devil can jump in and play upon the sentiment and perform his bait-and-switch technique.

The Devil's technique builds upon the sentiment. He latches hold of the "I *want* to do God's will but just can't" sentiment and validates it, "yes, it's true . . . you want to in your heart of hearts . . . it is sooo hard and there is too much on your plate already." Now comes the bait and switch, "God knows how hard it is, He doesn't want it to crush you. What He really wants is for you to do the best you can and don't let it get in the way of enjoying the life He gave you." Actually sounds pretty good, doesn't it? Yes it does, as most well-crafted lies do. It should also sound very familiar: "Has God really said that you should not eat it, ever, at all?" or "Throw yourself down. For it is written [didn't God say that], 'He will command his angels concerning you, and they will lift you up.'" The Devil tempts us to abandon doing God's will by suggesting that we have misunderstood God's wishes. He then suggests that all God really expects is for us to *want* to do His will. He then "proves" to us that God never really expected us to do *all* of His will *always* by arguing that we know that we want to but that we can't always do His will, so, of course, He knows this as well. Therefore, if God knows that we want to but can't, He must only be requiring us to want to do His will. He doesn't require us to do His will. It is a rather dazzling bit of demonic logic, and its premises are false, and its conclusion is invalid. But it sounds just like we want it to sound. It does the trick most of the time.

The final step is to substitute doing some other good thing in place of what we ought to be doing. The Devil will suggest doing something that we want to do. Here, our culture helps him. Our wants have been culturally conditioned to desire only the things that are bigger, better, and faster and cost me as little as possible. The Devil will suggest that God really wants you to enjoy! Go out and accomplish what you desire. That is God's will. Sure, go work at the soup kitchen on Thanksgiving morning, good . . . win-win . . . it's quick, you're done, no strings, no further commitments . . . win-win. This will be the death of us.

To live as Jesus lived, we must reject the idea that what we find desirable now is what God wants us to desire. We must train to develop a style of living that values the small positive changes God is making to our character. We train ourselves to desire God's approval over the meager fare of our immediate accomplishments.

Today's Exercises

Core Scripture: Matthew 4:8-9

Read aloud Matthew 4:8-9.

Recite this week's memory verses aloud five times.

> Therefore, as God's chosen people, holy and dearly loved, clothe yourselves with compassion, kindness, humility, gentleness and patience. (Colossians 3:12)

Meditate on today's passage.

Request to Be in His Presence

"Dear Lord, bring me into the context of Your world."

1. *Read it*—Remember: We read now only what is there, to hear once again, only what was spoken then.

   Read Matthew 4:8-9 at least twice, out loud.

2. *Think it*—select a portion, a phrase within the reading, and mull it over in your mind, thinking about the context and setting, reimagining the event, putting yourself into the situation. As you meditate, use all five senses to re-create the context and the setting by building the images that are supplied within the passages.

3. *Pray it*—ask God to give you understanding into how the truths He has spoken in these Scriptures apply to you now. Ask, "What is it about me that I need to deal with? What is it about me that must change?"

   Respond to God by accepting and admitting whatever responsibility is implied by what He has shown. Write what it is that God has shown you, and what you must admit responsibility for having done (or not done).

4. *Live it*—ask God to reveal to you what He wants you to do about what you have admitted.

List what particular action(s) you will take today to accomplish what God has revealed for you to do.

Pray, asking the Holy Spirit to empower you to act in obedience and to accomplish what He has revealed for you to do today.

Doing the Discipline: Preparing for the Five-Day Fast
Directing My Spirit's Passions Toward God

Today you will begin to direct your spirit's passion toward God in preparation for your fast.

List below the first three personal aspirations and personal goals that come to your mind.

My personal aspirations and goals:

Pray, Asking God to Direct Your Passions Toward Him

Ask God to help you lay aside whatever agenda you may have for meeting the needs you listed above. Ask Him to guide you through the journey of making His will the main passion in your life and to help you trust in Him.

Journal

Record ideas, impressions, feelings, questions, and any insights you may have had during today's time.

Prayer

Pray for each member of your community.

Being Led by the Crowd: Bowing to the Pressure of Impatience and Ambition

DAY SIX

Community Meeting

In preparation for this week's meeting, you will have read and reflected upon each of the week's five Core Thoughts, recorded your thoughts and observations, and are ready to recite this week's memory verses to the group.

WEEK SIX

Being Led by God from Temptation to Glory

DAY ONE

Prayer

Dear Lord, I lack a great deal of willpower when it comes to all kinds of temptations. I don't want to be such a pushover. I know that I have a willpower problem. I have enough willpower to decide not to do Your will. And I have enough willpower that when I want to do Your will, I usually want to do it the way I will. The problem with my willpower is that I don't seem to be able to use it to do Your will Your way. Please help me. I've been down this road many times. I'm tired. Amen.

Core Thought

> We have the power to overcome any temptation that God uses to transform us.

As we learned before, God uses temptations as occasions to do His transforming work and as opportunities to celebrate our transformation. His desire is to change us into disciples who will respond to temptations in the same way as did Jesus.

Jesus overcame temptation because He had trained Himself to be wholly dependent upon God's power to sustain Him, wholly dependent upon God's Word to form His understanding, and wholly dependent upon God's Spirit to cause the practice of doing God's will God's way to further grow His desire for doing only the will of God. We will also have the power to overcome any temptation once we have established the habits necessary to train us to conform our desires to God's will. To live as Jesus lived, we must overcome temptation by becoming wholly dependent on God's Word, God's power, and God's Spirit to lead us beyond temptation to glory.

Today's Exercises

Core Scripture: Matthew 4:10-11
Read aloud Matthew 4:10-11.
Recite this week's memory verses aloud five times.

> In this you greatly rejoice, though now for a little while you may
> have had to suffer grief in all kinds of trials. These have come
> so that your faith — of greater worth than gold, which perishes
> even though refined by fire — may be proved genuine and may
> result in praise, glory and honor when Jesus Christ is revealed.
> (1 Peter 1:6-7)

Meditate on today's passage.

Request to Be in His Presence

"Dear Lord, bring me into the context of Your world."

1. **Read it** — Remember: We read now only what is there, to hear once again, only what was spoken then.
   Read Matthew 4:10–11 at least twice, out loud.
2. **Think it** — select a portion, a phrase within the reading, and mull it over in your mind, thinking about the context and setting, reimagining the event, putting yourself into the situation. As you meditate, use all five senses to re-create the context and the setting by building the images that are supplied within the passages.
3. **Pray it** — ask God to give you understanding into how the truths He has spoken in these Scriptures apply to you now. Ask, "What is it about me that I need to deal with? What is it about me that must change?"

Respond to God by accepting and admitting whatever responsibility is implied by what He has shown. Write what it is that God has shown you, and what you must admit responsibility for having done (or not done).

4. *Live it*—ask God to reveal to you what He wants you to do about what you have admitted.

List what particular action(s) you will take today to accomplish what God has revealed for you to do.

Pray, asking the Holy Spirit to empower you to act in obedience and to accomplish what He has revealed for you to do today.

Doing the Discipline: Executing the Five-Day Fast

Beginning with today's first meal and continuing until the evening meal of Day Five, you will abstain from eating the first and second meals of the day. You may eat your evening or last meal of the day as usual, but you are to skip the morning and midday meals. During the entirety of the fast you may drink water, at any time. Remember to keep a journal of your experiences during your fast.

Journal

Record ideas, impressions, feelings, questions, and any insights you may have had during today's time.

Prayer

Pray for each member of your community.

Being Led by God from Temptation to Glory

DAY TWO

Prayer

Dear Lord, help me to know Your will when I must decide what to do, and help me to know how You would like Your will to be done. Dear Lord, open my mind's understanding to know what You have written in Your Word. Strengthen my heart's ability to recognize You as I experience You accomplishing Your will Your way through me and others. Amen.

Core Thought

> We obtain the knowledge to recognize temptation through the Word.

To endure and be victorious over temptation, we need to stand unfalteringly in the truth. To stand in the truth when we are tempted, we have to be able to discern the difference between the truth and the lie that has the appearance of being true. We see Jesus doing this very thing, and it resulted in His victory over the temptations of the Devil. To experience and celebrate the same kind of victory Jesus enjoyed, we need to discover and practice the same things that produced His ability to recognize the difference between the truth and the lies that masquerade as the truth.

The temptation account recalls how Jesus responded to each of the Devil's temptations. What was common in Jesus' responses is key to discovering what we must do to recognize truth from lies. The key lies in Jesus' recurring phrase, "It is written."

Jesus' responses indicated that He automatically tested all requests, claims, and proposals against the ultimate standard of truth, the Word of God. Jesus considered the written Word of God to be the exact expression of God's will and the exact description of how God's will was to be done: His will His way. Let's look at some interesting and instructive things about the dialog between the Devil and Jesus.

An interesting thing about the dialog is how little back-and-forth there is. You would think that there should be some real debate between the Devil and Jesus, but that is exactly what we do not see. There is only, "Do this," then, "It is written" then, "Do this . . . because it is written," then, "It is also written," then, "DO THIS," then, "Get away from me, Satan, because it is written." Why so little banter back and forth?

There is little debate because the Devil realized that no matter what approach or technique he used, Jesus' response was going to be the same. The Devil realized that Jesus was not going to engage in a debate about whose interpretation of Scripture accurately reflected God's will. Jesus knew the will of God and could confirm its truth in two ways: He knew what the Scriptures said and He could recognize the will of God when He heard it. How? He trained to be able to do so.

Jesus had trained in the Scriptures since He was young:

After three days they found him in the temple courts, sitting among the teachers, listening to them and asking them questions. Everyone who heard him was amazed at his understanding and his answers. (Luke 2:46-47)

Jesus had developed the ability to recognize God's will by practicing doing God's will:

I [Jesus] tell you the truth, the Son can do nothing by himself; he can do only what he sees his Father doing, because whatever the Father does the Son also does. For the Father loves the Son and shows him all he does." (John 5:19-20)

To live as Jesus lived, we must be able to distinguish the truth of God's will from anything else that pretends to be it. To do so means that we must train ourselves to know His will by knowing His Word. We will know His Word by knowing His Scriptures and by practicing doing His will His way.

Today's Exercises

Core Scripture: Matthew 4:10-11

Read aloud Matthew 4:10-11.

Recite this week's memory verses aloud five times.

> In this you greatly rejoice, though now for a little while you may
> have had to suffer grief in all kinds of trials. These have come
> so that your faith—of greater worth than gold, which perishes
> even though refined by fire—may be proved genuine and may
> result in praise, glory and honor when Jesus Christ is revealed.
> (1 Peter 1:6-7)

Meditate on today's passage.

Request to Be in His Presence

"Dear Lord, bring me into the context of Your world."

1. ***Read it***—Remember: We read now only what is there, to hear once again, only what was spoken then.

   Read Matthew 4:10-11 at least twice, out loud.

2. ***Think it***—select a portion, a phrase within the reading, mull it over in your mind, thinking about the context and setting, reimagining the event, putting yourself into the situation. As you meditate, use all five senses to re-create the context and the setting by building the images that are supplied within the passages.

3. ***Pray it***—ask God to give you understanding into how the truths He has spoken in these Scriptures apply to you now. Ask, "What

is it about me that I need to deal with? What is it about me that must change?"

Respond to God by accepting and admitting whatever responsibility is implied by what He has shown. Write what it is that God has shown you, and what you must admit responsibility for having done (or not done).

4. *Live it*—ask God to reveal to you what He wants you to do about what you have admitted.

List what particular action(s) you will take today to accomplish what God has revealed for you to do.

Pray, asking the Holy Spirit to empower you to act in obedience and to accomplish what He has revealed for you to do today.

Doing the Discipline: Continuing the Five-Day Fast
Documenting My Perspective During My Fasting

Journal

Record ideas, impressions, feelings, questions, and any insights you may have had during today's time.

Prayer

Pray for each member of your community.

Being Led by God from Temptation to Glory

DAY THREE

Prayer

Dear Father, I am sorry to say that sometimes I desire the thing I'm being tempted with more than I desire doing Your will. Help me to desire to do and have Your will done, more than I desire to have my will done. Amen.

Core Thought

We obtain the will to resist temptation through worship.

In war movies we often see repeated a familiar scene: soldiers who are about to be mobilized to where the fighting is fierce or soldiers who have been selected for what they and their commanding officers know will be a suicide mission are given a day or the night off or are allowed a last phone call to their loved ones. Invariably, someone makes the remark that this is being done "so that they will remember just what it is they are fighting for." And the truth is expressed well in the sentiment. It is a deep truth.

It is true that we will make all kinds of sacrifices, endure many hardships, and suffer greatly if we know that by doing so, we will accomplish something for the good of someone we love. When we value someone greatly, we will make great sacrifices for their sake. This is a deep truth, a foundational truth. We see the greatest expression of it in God's sacrifice of His only Son, Jesus, for our sake: "For God so loved the world that he gave his one and only Son, that whoever believes in him shall not perish but have eternal life" and, "What, then, shall we say in response to this? If God is for us, who can be against us? He who did not spare his own Son, but gave him up for us all—how will he not also, along with him, graciously give us all things?" (John 3:16; Romans 8:31-32, respectively).

To live as Jesus lived means to live so as to develop the will to always resist temptation. We develop our will to resist temptation by cultivating our desire for doing only God's will. We will cultivate the desire for doing only God's will when we value Him more that we value ourselves. How do we teach ourselves to value God more that ourselves? We do so by practicing a kind of behavior designed to train us to really believe that we value God above ourselves. The behavior that will teach us this is called sacrifice.

When we make a sacrifice of ourselves—placing all that we are and ever will be at His disposal to do with as He pleases—we are saying to Him that we love Him more than we love ourselves. This is what is meant by worship. It is by this sacrificial manner of worship that God transforms us:

> Therefore, I urge you, brothers, in view of God's mercy, to offer your bodies as living sacrifices, holy and pleasing to God—this is your spiritual act of worship. Do not conform any longer to the pattern of this world, but be transformed by the renewing of your mind. Then you will be able to test and approve what God's will is—his good, pleasing and perfect will. (Romans 12:1-2)

To live as Jesus lived means that we will always resist temptation because we have practiced sacrificing our own desires to do His will His way so much that our tastes have been transformed and can no longer be satisfied by anything sin's temptation has to offer.

Today's Exercises

Core Scripture: Matthew 4:10-11

Read aloud Matthew 4:10-11.

Recite this week's memory verses aloud five times.

> In this you greatly rejoice, though now for a little while you may have had to suffer grief in all kinds of trials. These have come so that your faith—of greater worth than gold, which perishes even though refined by fire—may be proved genuine and may result in praise, glory and honor when Jesus Christ is revealed. (1 Peter 1:6-7)

Meditate on today's passage.

Request to Be in His Presence

"Dear Lord, bring me into the context of Your world."

1. ***Read it***—Remember: We read now only what is there, to hear once again, only what was spoken then.

   Read Matthew 4:10-11 at least twice, out loud.

2. ***Think it***—select a portion, a phrase within the reading, and mull it over in your mind, thinking about the context and setting, reimagining the event, putting yourself into the situation. As you meditate, use all five senses to re-create the context and the setting by building the images that are supplied within the passages.

3. ***Pray it***—ask God to give you understanding into how the truths He has spoken in these Scriptures apply to you now. Ask, "What is it about me that I need to deal with? What is it about me that must change?"

   Respond to God by accepting and admitting whatever responsibility is implied by what He has shown. Write what it is that God has shown you, and what you must admit responsibility for having done (or not done).

4. *Live it*—ask God to reveal to you what He wants you to do about what you have admitted.

List what particular action(s) you will take today to accomplish what God has revealed for you to do.

Pray, asking the Holy Spirit to empower you to act in obedience and to accomplish what He has revealed for you to do today.

Doing the Discipline: Continuing the Five-Day Fast
Documenting My Perspective During My Fasting

Journal

Record ideas, impressions, feelings, questions, and any insights you may have had during today's time.

Prayer

Pray for each member of your community.

Being Led by God from Temptation to Glory

DAY FOUR

Prayer

Dear Lord, I don't mind doing things for other people, but sometimes I find myself thinking things that I know You don't like (in fact, I don't like me thinking them either). They usually boil down to wondering if the people I'm serving really appreciate the effort. If I think that they don't, it's very hard for me to want to help them again. Yes, I know that's bad. I'm sorry. Help me to change, please. Amen.

Core Thought

We obtain the strength to endure temptation through service.

Worshipping God grows in us the will to resist temptation. Serving God grows in us the strength and resolve to endure the suffering we will experience as we resist temptation. To live as Jesus lived we must develop the same kind of strength that Jesus exercised to enable us to endure temptation and bring God glory. But where did Jesus' strength to endure come from?

Jesus' power to endure came from a confidence in God that grew within him. Jesus' trust in His Father's love for Him grew due to His constant experience of God's power acting through others to meet His needs. He trusted that God loved Him and was confident that He would continue to provide for Him as He continued to serve His Father. Jesus had confidence in God's love and provision that grew in Him as a result of His personal experience of the power of God to provide when He was doing the Father's will by serving the people He loved.

To live as Jesus lived is to endure the suffering that comes with temptation through the strength that develops from our confidence in God's love for us and His ability to provide for us. This results from our experience of God's meeting our needs through the service of others and meeting other's needs by God's power acting through us in service to Him.

Today's Exercises
Core Scripture: Matthew 4:10-11
Read aloud Matthew 4:10-11.
Recite this week's memory verses aloud five times.

> In this you greatly rejoice, though now for a little while you may
> have had to suffer grief in all kinds of trials. These have come
> so that your faith—of greater worth than gold, which perishes
> even though refined by fire—may be proved genuine and may
> result in praise, glory and honor when Jesus Christ is revealed.
> (1 Peter 1:6-7)

Meditate on today's passage.

Request to Be in His Presence
"Dear Lord, bring me into the context of Your world."

1. **Read it**—Remember: We read now only what is there, to hear
   once again, only what was spoken then.
       Read Matthew 4:10-11 at least twice, out loud.
2. **Think it**—select a portion, a phrase within the reading, and mull
   it over in your mind, thinking about the context and setting,
   reimagining the event, putting yourself into the situation. As you
   meditate, use all five senses to re-create the context and the setting
   by building the images that are supplied within the passages.
3. **Pray it**—ask God to give you understanding into how the truths
   He has spoken in these Scriptures apply to you now. Ask, "What

is it about me that I need to deal with? What is it about me that must change?"

Respond to God by accepting and admitting whatever responsibility is implied by what He has shown. Write what it is that God has shown you, and what you must admit responsibility for having done (or not done).

4. *Live it* — ask God to reveal to you what He wants you to do about what you have admitted.

List what particular action(s) you will take today to accomplish what God has revealed for you to do.

Pray, asking the Holy Spirit to empower you to act in obedience and to accomplish what He has revealed for you to do today.

Doing the Discipline: Continuing the Five-Day Fast
Documenting My Perspective During My Fasting

164 LIVE as Jesus Lived

Journal

Record ideas, impressions, feelings, questions, and any insights
you may have had during today's time.

Prayer

Pray for each member of your community.

Being Led by God from Temptation to Glory

DAY FIVE

Prayer

Dear Lord, I do want to be like Jesus. Please help me to continue to practice the things that will help me accomplish this. Amen.

Core Thought

> To live as Jesus lived we must train ourselves to habitually act from the character and power of Christ that God is growing in us.

Studying the temptation of Jesus will have been worthwhile if we have understood some of the simple truths it presents.

First, when we follow God's leading doing His will His way and it leads us into situations where it appears that we will benefit by not doing God's will God's way, it is a sure sign that this is an occasion that God is using to transform us.

Second, take note of the sequence of events in this last exchange between Satan and Jesus.

After the Devil makes his offer, all the kingdoms in exchange for Jesus' worship, Jesus tells him to leave, the Devil obeys, and then angels came and attended Jesus. The second truth is that living as Jesus lived, doing God's will God's way, transforms us into the kind of disciple who, like Jesus, will not succumb to temptation by his body's appetites (turn stones to bread), his mind's ego (cast your self down), or by the influence of his culture (take the short cut and worship me). He can keep his commitments to God no matter the *kind* of temptation. And this leads to the next truth.

Third, Christians who train to make a habit of doing God's will God's way become disciples who can stand firm and keep their commitments to God no matter the *source* of the temptation. Once the habit of doing God's will God's way is set, there is little even the Devil himself can do to make you fall.

After refusing the Devil, Jesus tells him to leave. This is the first time Jesus has asked him to do so, and we should ask ourselves why so late in the game? Why didn't He tell him to leave earlier? The answer is very simple: one, Jesus is being obedient to God's leading, so He will not try to escape temptation but will endure it; two, He knows that no matter the source of temptation, only His choices can cause Him to fall; three, because He has trained Himself to do God's will, He is able to do it, and because He has trained His will to desire God's will, He wants to do it. The Devil's offers are no longer compelling temptations for Him. They are merely minor distractions. Jesus does not tell the Devil to leave until he commits blasphemy against God.

The last truth is that the disciple who has trained to desire and habitually do God's will God's way can endure any attack upon his own body, mind, or reputation. Like Jesus, he will not seek revenge for wrongs done to him. But he will act to the point of sacrificing all he has to oppose anything that attacks the honor due God's name or the honor of God's namesakes. The Devil who goes about as a roaring lion seeking whom he may devour realized he had roused the anger of the True Lion of the King of Judah (1 Peter 5:8). The text says that he "departed." In another place it adds "until an opportune time" (Luke 4:13, KJV). As we now know, there was to be no more opportune time. And so it is with a disciple who is trained to do God's will God's way, who lives as Jesus lived. There simply is no longer any opportunity for temptation. There are only opportunities to enjoy doing God's will His way.

Today's Exercises

Core Scripture: Matthew 4:10-11

Read aloud Matthew 4:10-11.

Recite this week's memory verses aloud five times.

> In this you greatly rejoice, though now for a little while you may
> have had to suffer grief in all kinds of trials. These have come
> so that your faith—of greater worth than gold, which perishes
> even though refined by fire—may be proved genuine and may
> result in praise, glory and honor when Jesus Christ is revealed.
> (1 Peter 1:6-7)

Meditate on today's passage.

Request to Be in His Presence

"Dear Lord, bring me into the context of Your world."

1. ***Read it***—Remember: We read now only what is there, to hear
   once again, only what was spoken then.

   Read Matthew 4:10-11 at least twice, out loud.

2. ***Think it***—select a portion, a phrase within the reading, and mull
   it over in your mind, thinking about the context and setting,
   reimagining the event, putting yourself into the situation. As you
   meditate, use all five senses to re-create the context and the setting
   by building the images that are supplied within the passages.

3. ***Pray it***—ask God to give you understanding into how the truths
   He has spoken in these Scriptures apply to you now. Ask, "What
   is it about me that I need to deal with? What is it about me that
   must change?"

   Respond to God by accepting and admitting whatever
   responsibility is implied by what He has shown. Write what it is
   that God has shown you, and what you must admit responsibility
   for having done (or not done).

4. *Live it*—ask God to reveal to you what He wants you to do about what you have admitted.

List what particular action(s) you will take today to accomplish what God has revealed for you to do.

Pray, asking the Holy Spirit to empower you to act in obedience and to accomplish what He has revealed for you to do today.

Doing the Discipline: Continuing the Five-Day Fast
Documenting My Perspective During My Fasting

Journal

Record ideas, impressions, feelings, questions, and any insights you may have had during today's time.

Prayer

Pray for each member of your community.

Being Led by God from Temptation to Glory

DAY SIX

Community Meeting

In preparation for this week's meeting, you will have read and reflected upon each of the week's five Core Thoughts, recorded your thoughts and observations, and are ready to recite this week's memory verses to the group.

Doing the Discipline: Breaking the Five-Day Fast
Deriving the Profit from My Fasting

Start by reviewing the journal entries that you made:

1. Read each statement and ask yourself, "What did I mean when I wrote this down?"
2. Using the space below, answer the question

"What did I experience?"

"What do I know now from these experiences?"

3. Ask the Lord the following questions and write whatever comes to your mind as the result.

   "Lord, what do you want me to learn from these experiences?"

   "Lord, what do you want me to do with what I now know?"

4. Write a short summary of what you experienced while preparing, executing, and breaking your five-day fast.

5. Write a short statement of what you learned and what you believe
   God is leading you to do with what you have learned from your fast.

ABOUT THE AUTHORS

BILL HULL's mission is to call the church to return to its disciple-making roots. He is a writer and discipleship evangelist calling the church to *choose the life*, a journey that Jesus called every disciple to pursue. This journey leads to a life of spiritual transformation and service. A veteran pastor, Bill has written ten books on this subject. In 1990 he founded T-NET International, a ministry devoted to transforming churches into disciple-making churches.

The core of Bill's writing is *Jesus Christ, Disciplemaker*; *The Disciple-Making Pastor*; and *The Disciple-Making Church*. He now spends his time helping leaders experience personal transformation so they can help transform their churches.

Bill and his wife, Jane, enjoy their not-so-quiet life, helping to raise their "highly energetic" grandchildren, in the beautiful Southern California sunshine.

PAUL MASCARELLA has served in local church ministry for more than twenty-five years as an associate pastor, minister of music, and worship director while holding an executive management position at a daily newspaper in Los Angeles, California. He is associate director of *Choose the Life Ministries*, where the abundance of his time and energy go to assisting churches as they embark on The *Choose the Life Journey*, and proceed forward with the EXPERIENCE THE LIFE series. He also serves on the Board of Directors for Bill Hull Ministries. He holds the Bachelor of Philosophy and Master of Theological Studies degrees.

Paul and his wife, Denise, reside in southern California.

Change from ordinary to Christlike.

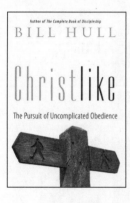